Education Reimagined

Education Reimagined

A Space for Risk

Ira David Socol
Cheryl (Walchack) Harris
J. Michael Thornton II

ROWMAN & LITTLEFIELD
Lanham • Boulder • New York • London

Published by Rowman & Littlefield
An imprint of The Rowman & Littlefield Publishing Group, Inc.
4501 Forbes Boulevard, Suite 200, Lanham, Maryland 20706
www.rowman.com

6 Tinworth Street, London SE11 5AL, United Kingdom

Copyright © 2019 by Ira David Socol, Cheryl (Walchack) Harris, and J. Michael Thornton II

All rights reserved. No part of this book may be reproduced in any form or by any electronic or mechanical means, including information storage and retrieval systems, without written permission from the publisher, except by a reviewer who may quote passages in a review.

British Library Cataloguing in Publication Information Available

Library of Congress Cataloging-in-Publication Data

Names: Socol, Ira, author. | Harris, Cheryl Ann, 1960– author. | Thornton, John Michael, II, 1978– author.
Title: Education reimagined : a space for risk / Ira David Socol, Cheryl Ann Harris, John Michael Thornton II.
Description: Lanham, Maryland : Rowman & Littlefield, 2019. | Includes bibliographical references.
Identifiers: LCCN 2018043503 (print) | LCCN 2018045188 (ebook) | ISBN 9781475828573 (Electronic) | ISBN 9781475828559 (cloth : alk. paper) | ISBN 9781475828566 (pbk. : alk. paper)
Subjects: LCSH: Classrooms—Planning. | Classroom environment. | Space (Architecture)
Classification: LCC LB3325.C5 (ebook) | LCC LB3325.C5 S64 2019 (print) | DDC 371.6/21—dc23
LC record available at https://lccn.loc.gov/2018043503

∞ ™ The paper used in this publication meets the minimum requirements of American National Standard for Information Sciences Permanence of Paper for Printed Library Materials, ANSI/NISO Z39.48-1992.

Printed in the United States of America

Contents

Preface		vii
Introduction		ix
1	A Risk Worth Taking	1
2	Getting Started	13
3	Creating a Learning Space	23
4	Teacher Autonomy	33
5	Growth Mind-Set	45
6	Creating a Vision	61
7	Sharing the Vision	71
8	Changing the Learning Space	81
9	Financial Awareness	91
10	Radical Leadership	99
11	Decision-Making: Choice and Comfort	107
12	The Learning Space and Student Autonomy in the Classroom	115
13	A Different Vision of Risk: Differentiation and Individualism in the Classroom	125
14	Elementary School Learning Spaces	139
15	Middle School Learning Spaces	147
16	High School Learning Spaces	157
About the Authors		167

Preface

Do you think the classroom is a place for creativity and critical thinking? Do you want classrooms to be flexible learning spaces that enable students the opportunity to move freely throughout the room? Shouldn't students have the chance to make critical decisions in the classroom with respect to their own education? Do you want to gently break away from traditional teaching and learning experiences and demonstrate a growth mind-set to give all students and teachers the best learning opportunity? If so, *Education Reimagined: A Space for Risk* is a must-read for you.

Over the course of our careers, we have been blessed with many mentors. For each of us, we have soaked up the advice we have been given while taking risks to challenge ourselves to better our students' educational experience. An entire chapter in this book could be dedicated to our mentors and the vast knowledge gained from each. There is one who had a profound impact on all three of us. We acknowledge Dr. Pam Moran, superintendent of Albemarle County Public Schools (recently retired), as an inspiration and supporter of teachers and learning. It is her vision for all learners that prompted and compelled us to explain what's best for kids and to write this book.

As you read through this book, you will read about many ideas and techniques to help create a comfortable space for students. Furthermore, as you read about making choices and taking risks, you will hear some ideas repeated. These are intentional repeats to help you as you attempt to create a learning environment where students learn how to learn by taking risks, at the same time feeling safe while moving forward on their personal learning journey. We challenge you to swim in the waters of research and proven best practices of choice and comfort. Dive in deep or doggie-paddle. The choice is yours.

Once a new strategy or concept has been introduced, it is all about the students and you are the "guide on the side!" Allow your students the freedom to spread their tentacles of curiosity and soak up more lifelong learning skills than you could ever imagine in the ocean of knowledge. Jump in or test the water and observe your ideas taking shape for your own teaching and learning experiences.

Introduction

We began our careers on separate educational journeys, but the common thread across all three of our careers has been a fierce commitment to ensure the learners we teach are at the center of every decision we make. When our paths first crossed, the school district in which we work had just experienced the Great Recession. However, instead of seeing our progressive work diminished by loss of funding, teachers and administrators were collaborating to take our long-standing commitment to lifelong learning competencies to the next level.

We found ourselves connected through our common passion that *all* learners gain access to the tools, resources, experiences, learning spaces, and curriculum they need to be successful, not just in school, but for life. As we ventured together more deeply into social media, through Twitter chats, blogs, YouTube, Skype, and Google Hangouts, we discovered others all over the world who were on similar journeys to create a multitude of learning paths for students. We became connected teachers and learners, and, in doing so, we began to deeply transform and purposefully redesign our teaching places into learning spaces.

Ira took on the role of our chief provocateur—asking tough questions, pushing us to consider different points of view, and connecting us to the idea that natural learning environments did not look like or function as traditional classrooms of twentieth-century American schools. We took on roles of learning and leading designers, architects, and engineers who were willing to experiment with new ways of situating space, resources, materials, tools, and teaching that allowed all students to show us their strengths and assets. While we have always believed in our power as educators to make a difference, to be creative problem solvers, and to build caring relationships with students, we suddenly found ourselves questioning the parameters that defined schooling as we have known it across our careers.

The concept of equity became a constant in our conversations together, and as we deeply considered the differences and diversity among the learners in our care, we questioned the efficacy of mass standardization of content, tests, and teaching strategies that have permeated public education throughout this century's accountability movement. Our conversations led us to experimental designs for learning that embraced the diversity of our students' capabilities, their preferences for how they wanted and needed to learn, and the many different media options that they wanted to use as tools to demonstrate their progress to us. Our classrooms became true "melting pots" of diversity, and we saw our students come to appreciate each other through their emotional, social, cognitive, and cultural dimensions as never before in our careers.

We have made changes to the design of our classrooms, creating a variety of options for seating even as we have helped our students find comfort in how they choose to work as individuals and teams. We have created a continuum of options for deeper learning through maker-infused curriculum, project-problem-passion-driven learning, universal design for learning accessibility tools and strategies, interactive and connected technologies, and our own increased instructional tolerance for the choices that students not only make but need to be successful as learners.

Our work has been challenging and sometimes challenged. However, when we reflect upon the stories of students, especially those with risk factors of poverty, attention, culture, and special needs, who have been set free as learners, we feel affirmed in our own efficacy. We have seen students from kindergarten to twelfth grade discover that their voices matter, personal agency gives them power in learning, and they can influence their peers, their school community, and even the world. We believe you will find this theme of voice, agency, and influence across every chapter of our book.

We ourselves, and other teachers located near us, have felt our sense of empowerment grow through our interactions with each other. We immediately felt a bond of kinship in our work as educators as we considered all the ways our students needed us to shift learning power from us to them. This began the first time Ira asked Michael the question, "Why can't they do their work together *under* the tables?" or his challenge to students in Cheryl's class to write about something that was hard to share from their own lives even as they considered the impact of the Holocaust on the lives of those who lived through it.

Michael can describe the impact on him as a teacher in watching the empowered learning efficacy of his third-grade class unfold as they took their twenty sheets of paper tower-building challenge out to classes around the world and then raptly watched Twitter and their Google Doc explode with the kinetic energy of kids from Ireland to Chicago attempt to outbuild each other by creating the tallest paper tower ever.

Cheryl can share story after story of students who after years in school finally developed personal confidence as writers because she removed the constraints of what it means to write in school according to formula, tool, or topic. Then, as her students became collaborative project designers and presenters, these same students who had never seen themselves as capable writers, or as able to share their work publicly, generated some of the most powerful projects and writing that she has ever experienced in her classes.

As you begin chapter 1, we encourage you to consider that the per-student resources of our district are the average for the nation. We all have worked in schools with few at-risk students and ones where more than one in two students lives in poverty. Our students have come to us from urban, rural, and suburban homes. They all have needs—different needs—but as we have created space for risk, we have found that a student from a middle-class family may be less likely to take learning risks than one living in poverty. Yet, by creating our own spaces for risk, we have discovered assets and strengths in all our students that support them to be risk takers in their learning. We also have found that it's only when dissonance is created in what we believe, value, and know that our learners grow and so do we.

Thank you for taking the risk to purchase our book. We encourage you to reach out to us with your questions and thoughts. We continue on our journey, and no matter how far apart life may take us, we will forever be together—and you can always find us on Twitter!

Ira David Socol @irasocol
Cheryl (Walchack) Harris @peacefulsmile
J. Michael Thornton II @mthornton78

Chapter One

A Risk Worth Taking

> *I speak to everyone in the same way, whether he is the garbage man or the president of the university.* —Albert Einstein

QUESTIONS TO PONDER IN THIS CHAPTER

- *How can you demonstrate that you trust and respect students?*
- *How do you offer choice within their classroom?*
- *What does comfort look like with students, work habits, and furniture choice and placement?*

WHERE TO BEGIN?

A person must be trusted before that person gains the respect of learners. You cannot assume that each student who enters your classroom has been taught respect or, as a matter of fact, has been *shown* what respect looks like. Respect comes with relationships that are grounded in a sense of regard for students, regardless of the challenges they may bring with them into our classroom. Compliance differs from respect.

Students in a compliance-driven classroom may follow rules or do what they are directed to do by the teacher because they have been taught to be compliant or out of fear of punishment. Respect emerges as students come to believe that their voice matters and that they are trusted in their learning agency. This may happen easily for some students and be more difficult for others. Some students mistrust because it's a learned behavior from negative experiences with adults in school—or out. We believe that building trust begins with modeling of respect toward students as individuals through body language, tone of voice, and use of language.

How should you speak to your students? Does your tone of voice give the message you intend? Consider recording yourself (using a cell phone or other recording device) and then listen to it later in the day. Is your tone of voice respectful? Do you use the same tone for each student? Do you model respect in the language you use so that students hear what respect looks like? Role-play scenarios, especially during the first couple of weeks of school or after a long vacation, so students begin to see what respect looks like in their classroom with other students and with you.

Reinforce students for what they do that represents your class's norms. The most effective feedback happens in close proximity to an action by a student and includes specifics of the behavior being reinforced. We know that students respond to us when we provide them with positive reinforcement about their behavior, their work ethic, their work with others, and their assistance with work in class.

This kind of reinforcement, or specific praise, sets the tone for how students will interact with each other and resources in class. It also shapes the behavior of students who may struggle with staying within class norms or who simply do not know the norms—yet (Saaris 2016).

For example, if students are challenged to gather all the necessary materials needed for class before they begin their work, provide the learner with specific reinforcement for doing that. However, also remember from the research on praise that simply saying "Good job" isn't enough. It's important to note specifically what the student did. "Thank you for being ready for class with your materials" suffices.

Maintaining our own tolerance throughout each day, throughout each class, is critical to build a culture of respect. After all, isn't that what we expect students to do? We all need to demonstrate trust and respect throughout the entire day. That's sometimes hard for us too.

In class, you are the model in the room, and as the model it's important to show what it looks like to listen to others. When a student responds within the class, hear the student out. Take the time for peers to reflect along with the student whether he or she is on the right path. Modeling how to respond with respect is critical and something you have to coach among students to create an inclusive community that regards its members. When a student reflectively processes a response with another classmate, it places that student in a position of trustworthiness in sharing feedback.

When you demonstrate to students how important it is to wait your turn to speak, then it says everyone's time is of value. Allocating the same amount of time to talk and encouraging each learner to feel comfortable to share is a function of your classroom guidance, support, and leadership.

Sometimes one student may monopolize the discussion. If you see that happening with a student repeatedly, it is worth the time to meet privately to discuss that. Some students are unaware of how much they talk, often be-

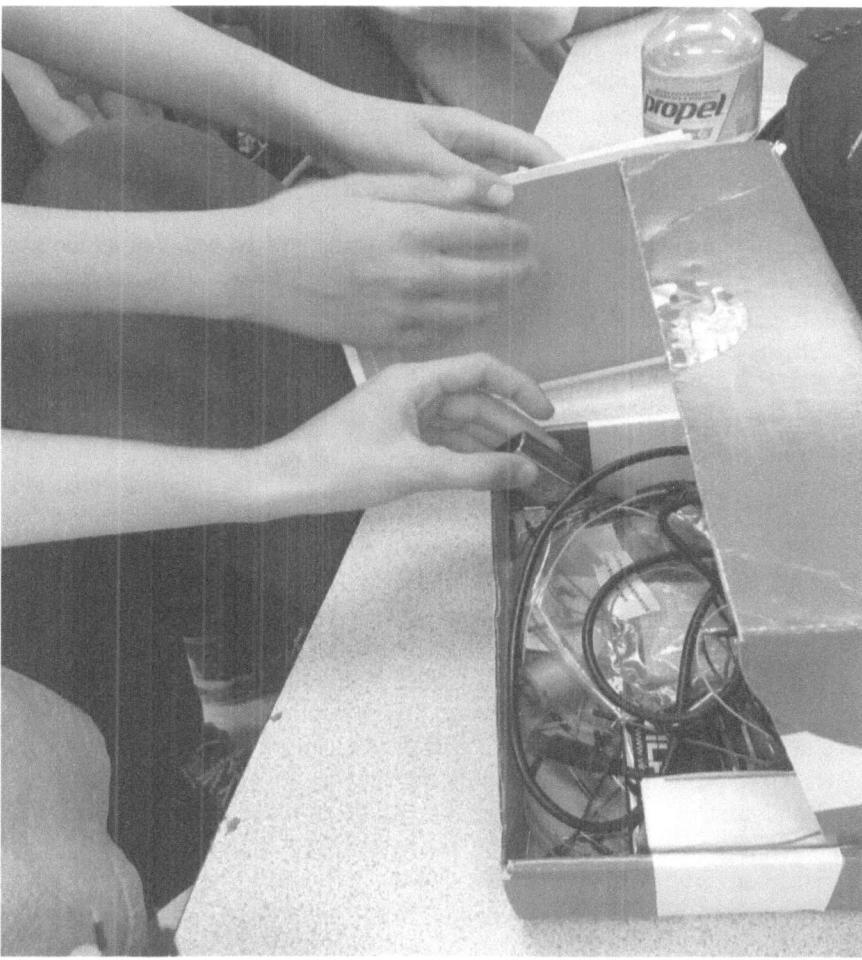

cause they want to show what they know or they simply are auditory processors. However, listening is a key skill to working with others in life. You might use a timer to help the entire class develop a temporal understanding of how much time they talk as individuals (Levi 2015).

We also believe that students are there to help you build a positive culture in the classroom, and this comes from how they interact with each other. Model complimenting others on a regular basis, and your students will follow suit in no time. If you drop something on the floor, make sure you pick it up. If you walk past a student and unintentionally knock that student's papers on the floor, pick them up and apologize. Be courteous toward students. They will, in turn, demonstrate this behavior to both the teacher and other students. The teacher's expectations should remain high, but attainable, in this social and emotional learning space.

Practice random acts of kindness in and out of the classroom. When students consistently observe you being respectful to others, they will, in turn, follow your actions. For some students it may take a while to reciprocate, and some may never praise another aloud. Hopefully, though, they will begin to positively engage with peers in some quiet way or gesture. It is also important that you model polite language even as you expect your students to do the same: "Please," "Thank you," and "Excuse me." How you treat others is how they should expect to be treated.

TRUST AND RESPECT

Allow students to stand in front of the class and review a concept, using your or their own notes. Allow them to take a risk in their classroom, which is a safe zone. Yours is the classroom where no one laughs at each other, but instead each student assists others. Give students opportunities in which to demonstrate trust. Talk about trust and how it affects learning. Allow students to raise their hand and give a wrong answer. No one in the room should laugh, but instead encourage how peers can arrive at the correct answer.

Empower your students to think for themselves or know how to locate the correct answer. Encourage students to "learn how to learn" and be involved in class discussions, where it's safe in the classroom to be incorrect sometimes. Give them time to research the correct answer. They will feel empowered and part of the group. Encourage students to lead class discussions. They will follow the model you set and sometimes surprise everyone.

This can happen in class activities too. We've seen this happen when a student in class who seldom has had opportunities to successfully show what he or she can do gets a chance to be seen by peers in a positive way. For example, a student who struggled with math on paper was able to help peers make a cardboard trebuchet, and then the team learned how to conduct trials to find the average distance they could "shoot" a paper ball from it. Another student with artistic talents became the designer for a team mural that illustrated what they had identified as the pivotal scene in a book. When you look for and support opportunities to advantage children's strengths as learners, then they begin to see themselves as regarded by you and others as an asset to the community.

You also earn students' trust by demonstrating respect and by planning work that is meaningful. If students can demonstrate that they are knowledgeable about how to write a paragraph, then you can move them to more

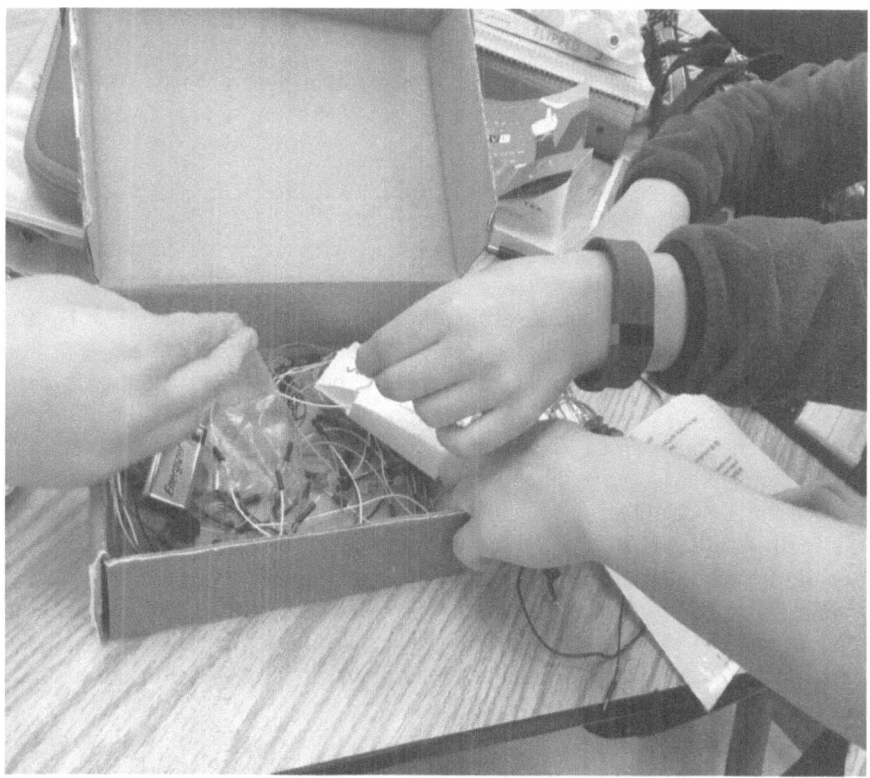

challenging and meaningful activities. Challenge their minds. Stretch their imaginations.

If a student has been absent and has missed valuable writing time, will he or she be able to demonstrate the concept the class is learning in three brief pieces of writing? Sometimes, you will need to differentiate time. This may look like giving a different assignment that will engage the learning in practicing and understanding the concept with an end in mind of catching up after being absent. By setting up alternative assignments, you show respect for the students' time. In turn, students show knowledge of the concept. We think this is a win-win situation.

Demonstrating trust creates a perspective among learners that you care. This helps build confidence in students, which allows them the freedom to explore and create. Trusting students allows them to be independent. They know the routines of their class, and when you allow students the freedom to choose a group, rubric, task, and/or audience, you are demonstrating your trust in them. Independence is shaped by allowing students to make choices.

It's sometimes a struggle for any of us who teach to shift the control and power to students by giving them choices, but when that happens, learners often exceed our expectations.

Building inclusive communities of respect brings us to two important activities of the year: Back-to-School Night and student-led conferences.

TAKING CONTROL

Back-to-School Night

Back-to-School Night occurs within the first two weeks of the school year. This is when teachers usually share the curriculum, class routines, behavior expectations, grading practices, homework expectations, et cetera with parents. Ask students who can stay after school that evening, and have the four or so students develop a PowerPoint, Prezi, or any other presentation method the students choose that can be used to share information with parents.

We think that planning to engage parents in that first community interaction with families is key to setting up their support of their children and you during the school year. Begin by introducing yourself to parents by sharing your own brief biography and philosophy of teaching and learning. Use a student team to show and explain the expectations in their room to the parents. Then you can wrap it up by asking if there are any questions on a topic, perhaps something the students didn't cover.

Take the time to listen to parents, answer their questions, and hand the parents a business card and syllabus/pacing guide on the way out. How impressed will those parents be hearing what you expect from the students in only the second week of school? Back-to-School Night that involves students in the presentation sends the message that you intend to make the school year all about their children as learners.

Student-Led Conferences

Another time students thoroughly enjoy taking charge is during parent conferences. Parent conferences occur near the beginning of the school year. Have the students run their own student-led conferences, but remember to structure the process around the outcomes the student wants, those you want, and also what parents want to see as accomplishments (Hinton et al. 2014). You will need to set a few mandatory expectations (daily routine, read a choice of one of their pieces of writing, conferencing behaviors, and how to share at least three pieces of their best work with their parents).

We would suggest you begin this process by asking students to create a rubric based on how they want to share (e.g., iMovie, PowerPoint, comic strip illustrations, a children's book). Then they begin, in class, to create their own presentations. While each student is different and has a different style of sharing information with their parents, the outcome is that parents will see growth, understand what students are learning, and leave with a positive perspective that their child is developing not just content knowledge and skills but also competencies for life.

Students will need to practice with each other throughout the week to be prepared to run their parent conference. This is where misconceptions may be corrected from student to student. Also, remember to send a letter ahead of time to parents, explaining the sign-up process and that this will take approximately ten minutes, and to ask if they can send a baked or bought item in with their child that day. If they have questions, encourage them to email you.

Once you are known for conducting student-led conferences, the word gets out and parents of siblings begin to look forward to student-led conferences the following years as well. Not only do you build community in your own class, but you also are modeling a practice that other teachers can adopt.

On Student-Led Conference Night, we think it's important to create a context for building relationships among parents and students. Consider putting out punch in a punch bowl, some cups and napkins, a tablecloth, and a portion of the food items that the students brought that morning on a small table, and the rest set aside, in plain view, to set out as the night progresses. When you stand by the door and greet the students and families as they enter, they will feel you are greeting them almost as if they are entering your home.

The students choose where in the room they want to present. You can choose to have students pull the chairs out for their guests or not. The student then asks if anyone would like something to drink or eat. (They have been taught to keep food and drink away from electronics, so they will politely ask their family to do so as well.) Several presentations occur at a time.

Each family listens to their child present about their current progress in the class. The student runs through their presentation, while the parents and family members eat, watch, and ask questions or offer comments. The conversations you hear while children are presenting often homes in on what a student sees as successes or areas for growth. For example, a parent might say, "You don't always bring materials to class? Why is that?" The student might respond by stating they need additional supplies. These conversations form an important dialogue between family members.

Where is the teacher, you ask? The teacher is the "guide on the side!" There are eight conferences usually occurring at once in a classroom set up in groups for cooperative learning. As the student finishes, the parents will often just gush over their child's presentation. That gives you the opportunity to walk over and ask if the parents have any concerns or questions. They usually don't because you've already discussed any concerns on the telephone with them as the year has progressed.

Some parents excuse their child and ask the teacher to tell them how they are "really" doing. We've learned to respond with, "Just as your child stated, they need to bring all needed supplies to class, but if it starts to become a pattern I'll call or email you." We've found that very few parents will ask you questions on the side, if at all.

In fact, when you walk over to listen in to the conference, parents usually say, "Nope! I don't have any questions as my son/daughter already told me everything." Some students may come in with their football uniform on, face made up from drama practice, or with their instrument from band practice. In doing so, they send the message that they are comfortable in their classroom and they are ready to present to their family because it is safe to take risks.

Prior to the conference, the students should have the opportunity to role-play their presentation. They will take the presentation really seriously. On the day after student-led conferences, take the time in class to tell students that you enjoyed meeting or seeing their families again and that they did a wonderful job presenting. Then pass out the rubric with comments on them that were recorded by you when students were presenting. Tell students that this rubric belongs on their fridge. You will be surprised how many students go home and hang it up on their fridge.

If you are wondering about those students whose parents can't make it, we have a plan for that too. As you hand out the graded rubrics, hand them their blank ones. If you can line up staff, you might have the librarian or administrator present in the library to hear those presentations and place checks on the rubric.

You then can suggest to that group that they present to their family at home as well. This gives the student lots of choices, control through which they can demonstrate responsibility, trust, and respect with the teacher and their family, and most of all, the confidence necessary to take risks.

CHOICE IN SEATING

Should you let students sit where they want? We think so. Tell the students, "Sit where you will work the hardest." They walk around the room. Students will try the variety of chairs in the room: a papasan chair, couch, a regular student chair, a cushioned chair, a beanbag, a stool—but then usually go back to the first seat they tried. If you say, "New seats" about once every three weeks, you will find that students will begin to connect with students they might not meet otherwise. In our classrooms, students are not late to class, nor are they running, because they can choose and change their seat at any time.

If a student is not working or is stopping you from teaching because they are in a sidebar conversation with their friend, you will need to make eye contact with that student. When direct instruction on the concept is complete, the students may talk while they work but not share answers. If you are talking with the class and some students are talking, you will need to address that. You might simply walk over to those students and whisper, "I saw that you were talking when I was talking." The student may need to choose a new seat for the day because he or she stopped the flow of learning.

You might also pull the student aside for a private conversation to ask, "When a student presents in front of the class, do I talk?" Their response is of course, "No!" Ask who was affected by their conversation. They usually will just say themselves. Then they think of it and realize that the person with whom they were speaking and also those around them were affected. If you find that this is happening with multiple students, this could end up as a topic for class meetings.

We believe that the most important goal for students in our classrooms is that each is engaged and grows socially, academically, and emotionally. We model that we are not "out to get them" or "looking for them doing wrong." Instead, we focus on finding students doing what is right and build on that. That can happen in multiple ways. For example, when it is time to rearrange the room, we might move all the furniture off to the side and ask students to create illustrations by themselves or in a group (their choice) of where each piece of furniture should be placed. They vote on it, move it, make alterations, look for safety concerns, and move it again.

Even throughout the day, there will be adjustments. They arrive at strategic places for the octagon, small round, small square, and one rectangular table. Each of these tables has a "cushioned teacher's chair" or a few regular student chairs or stools. We find that when kids begin to understand that we care that all students are safe, learning, and respectful to each other, they begin to behave that way too.

After the room is rearranged, we make sure they know they can be in all of these in a comfy space they have created. Sometimes, if a student has a headache or just wants to be alone for a bit, they can sit somewhere else that they are comfortable. It's just not an issue! Each student feels safe enough to take a risk on where to sit, which assignment to do first, or which book to read (Merrill 2018).

CHOICE IN CURRICULAR ACTIVITIES: BUILDING INTEREST IN READING

Using an activity that provides choice for the class might start with something like a forty-book challenge. (The number can be altered to meet the needs of each student.) We begin this activity by stating how many books per genre will be read and that students should plan to read at least ten books per nine weeks. (The number may vary due to the length of the book.) Students choose which book they read, as well as the genre, and record the books in a log so that they can keep track.

During class, if you try this activity you might approach a student during silent reading time. (If there is a meeting for writing, it is during writing time.) In a composition book (tabs separate for each class), date the day under the student's name, ask for the title of the book they are reading and what page number they're on, and then ask a few concept questions that have been covered with support answers from the text. For example, you might ask if there was any foreshadowing in this book. The students answer either yes or no and give an example.

As you consider standards to be taught, you might include questions that ask about protagonists, the types of characters in the book, and how they know that's the type it is. It's about a three-minute conversation before moving to another student. This way you can teach the concept to the entire class while asking critical thinking questions one on one to hear students' answers. Concepts are also taught through the use of a poem, a newspaper article that students have read that day, or a short story. Gone are the days in which all students read the same novel or go for weeks on end with little student choice.

When it comes to students becoming better readers by having some choice in the matter, they will have ample opportunity to learn what they will need to meet the goals set for them. Students have choices to make.

Having created a trusting and respectful atmosphere in your classroom, students will be able to make choices in seating, group, rubric, product, and audience. If students make a few mistakes along the way, it's better they make them with the teacher present, guiding them through, than on their own, without any assistance.

Putting as much structural change as possible in place to shift power from teacher to student is key to creating a climate where it is safe for students to take risks in their class (Rimm-Kaufman and Sandilos 2011). We see improvement in individual student performance especially when learners have worked in a culture that supports collaboration, communication, and citizenship. This occurs because of ongoing support to model lifelong learning.

We've learned how to build in structures to support teachers to learn new strategies for use in a project-based environment. These structures include professional development, instructional coaching, and support for technology integration. When teachers and building-level principals work together to build trust and respect within the culture, it means that students will have many opportunities over time to learn.

WORKS CITED

Hinton, James, Don Kilburn, Marian Oswald, George Jones, Adam Gutierrez, and Shawn McCusker. 2014. "A Guide to Student-Led Conferences." Edudemic. December 18, 2014 http://www.edudemic.com/guide-to-student-led-conferences/.

Levi, Carolyn M. 2015. "Teacher Talk vs. Student Talk." Carolyn M. Levi. https://sites.google.com/a/csuglobal.edu/carolyn-levi/otl-560-facilitating-learning-and-transfer/teacher-talk-vs-student-talk.

Merrill, Stephen. 2018. "Flexible Classrooms: Research Is Scarce, But Promising." Edutopia. George Lucas Educational Foundation. https://www.edutopia.org/article/flexible-classrooms-research-scarce-promising.

Rimm-Kaufman, Sara, and Lia Sandilos. 2011. "Improving Students' Relationships with Teachers to Provide Essential Supports for Learning." American Psychological Association. Accessed July 8, 2018. www.apa.org/education/k12/relationships.aspx#.

Saaris, Natalie. 2016. "Effective Feedback for Deeper Learning." Actively Learn. June 2, 2016. https://www.activelylearn.com/post/effective-feedback-for-deeper-learning.

Chapter Two

Getting Started

The secret of getting ahead is getting started.—Mark Twain

QUESTIONS TO PONDER IN THIS CHAPTER

- *How can teachers begin the journey toward adapting their instructional practice in the classroom?*
- *What should be the first step toward change?*
- *What happens if the changes I make don't work?*
- *What resources or opportunities are available to allow a smooth transition?*

IN THE BEGINNING

As this chapter begins, it should be clear from the start that there is no one set path to change. The journey will not be the same for all, but it must start somewhere. The challenge is to start. That, by itself, is a big step. The acknowledgment that a change needs to happen can be one of the toughest hurdles to overcome.

Students deserve the very best education, and in order for that to be possible, educators must be willing to step out of their comfort zone to move forward. This chapter will discuss ways in which teachers such as you can push through the web that keeps them entangled in the status quo.

Undoubtedly, there are times the status quo is acceptable and permissible, but it can, and often does, become a safety net for those who are scared to try something new. For example, there are times when direct instruction—the dominant teaching strategy of the twentieth-century classroom—is still appropriate to use such as when you are teaching a new concept. However, direct instruction should be, in our opinion, used sparingly and in small doses. We are firm believers that the more we talk as teachers, the less engaged our learners become.

When we began to write this book together, we asked ourselves what we consider to be a key question relevant to shifting a community of learners from compliance-driven to student-centered learning. *Can a space for risk be created if the teacher in the room is not modeling that behavior?* The first step can be small. In fact, the first step should be small. Trying to accomplish too much at one time can be detrimental to the process. Even though a first step is small, the impact it can have on the classroom and the direction of future instructional practice is enormous (Edutopia 2015).

LOOK IN THE MIRROR

A mirror is an everyday instrument used in a variety of ways with multiple purposes. It is common practice to glance at a mirror when walking past one or to stop at a mirror to quickly fix a piece of clothing or a strayed hair. But what happens when someone truly stops and looks intently into the mirror? How does their perspective change? Will they see items missed at a quick glance? What will their reaction be to this new discovery?

Self-evaluation is difficult. It can lead to a mix of emotions. Some of those emotions can be positive while others could be negative. No matter how difficult it can be, self-evaluation is a necessary aspect of lifelong learning. For countless reasons, educators are deeply involved and invested in their profession.

However, we often have little time to self-reflect. We've worked both with peers in professional learning communities and with formal instructional coaches and learned that taking the time to reflect with another educator is key to us delving into what is working—or not—in our own classrooms. When a student is struggling academically or perhaps with behaviors that are inappropriate, we believe the first step is to ask, "What am I doing?"

We've learned that beginning with what we control allows us to consider what a learner needs from us to be successful. However, that's only the beginning of self-reflection. We may pull from our observations or even talk to other teachers who work with a student who has difficulty academically to find out if they see similar patterns.

Sometimes, we have discovered that a student, with whom one of us is having difficulty, is actually doing well in another class. This gives a starting point to ask why the student is struggling in one class and not in another. It could be that my relationship with the student is not as strong as it needs to be or that the content being taught in my class is less accessible for some reason. Or it may be that the strategies being used are not providing the level of engagement, practice, or focus that the student needs. Working with a trusted peer or coach serves as a mirror through which questions, feedback, and analysis of a specific student case study can inform next steps to change strategies or actions to build relationships ("Instructional Coaching," n.d.).

An educator's classroom is like another home. It is a place of comfort, control, choice, and creativity. Investment and control over the space can enable teachers to have a powerful impact on the students and the learning happening in the classroom. It also can make it difficult for teachers to acknowledge that a change needs to be made.

Teachers are developing multiple lesson plans a day and witnessing them in action. For any educator, seeing his or her lesson plans in action can be very powerful. However, it's easy to put blindfolds on and only see the positive of each and every lesson without delving deeper into the practices that are leading to less learning. Another strategy that can help make what you do in the classroom more transparent in the self-reflection process involves videotaping your classroom, even with your cell phone and an inexpensive tripod.

Doing so can be eye opening when you take the time to watch what occurs during a lesson. You can do this by yourself or with a peer or coach. Take the time to tally how often you interact with each student in the video. This can provide insight into your own interactions. Write down the questions you ask and consider what the purpose of the question is and does it lead to higher or lower levels of thinking.

In some cases, you may find your lessons and procedures push students away from a natural motivation to learn. The good news is you have control over that. The first step is to stop at the mirror and look. Not glance, but truly analyze. It will not be easy, but it can be a rewarding practice. We've shared a few examples of how you can look in the mirror. That's the easy part. The challenge is what to do next with your reflections. The next step is to change.

One example of change that we can share is our use of project-based learning (PBL) strategies. We have always used projects to engage learners.

However, there is a big difference between making projects, such as whole-class dioramas on biomes to engage learners, and doing a project-based learning unit in which students are able to study biomes, pick a research focus on something they want to impact, and then map and implement a learning project that will make a difference in their community ("Doing Projects vs. Project Based Learning PBL" 2016).

A PBL could be a mind-to-hands-on project such as placing environmental signage along a community nature trail or building an advocacy platform to lobby a local political entity to build a local ordinance to protect streams from runoff. When students participate in shaping projects, they often discover interests they did not even know about, and their engagement rises. But

we also see increased agency and a sense of being able to influence others through PBLs that class projects just don't generate.

Our reflections on project versus project-based learning and our willingness to dig in on professional learning led us to change practice. That's often not easy, but it is certainly rewarding when we get to observe students develop a "fire in the belly" for learning driven by questions, curiosities, and interests.

THE CHANGE: SEEING IS BELIEVING

It is an amazing time for educators. No longer do educators need to be isolated from their peers. In the past, teachers arrived at their classroom, closed their doors, and went to work. They rarely left their room and kept their students with them for most of the day. This is not to say creativity wasn't happening.

It surely was, but regardless of how much learning was happening or how engaged the students were, only those students inside the classroom and their teacher knew about it. What about the students next door? Were they experiencing a similar lesson? How was their educational experience? What if that wall between the classrooms was taken down? How would the students experience change? How would the instructional experience change?

All over the world, teachers are doing incredible activities in their classrooms. Social media has enabled educators to see past the four walls of their classrooms to view learning spaces all over the world. Apps such as Skype, Twitter, Instagram, Pinterest, YouTube, and Facebook today help educators see what is possible. These virtual professional learning network (PLN) connections can empower teachers to try something different. Seeing or hearing about another teacher's amazing lesson or watching a YouTube video of a PBL can be a deciding motivator to change.

For example, Michael has an amazing story about a class of third graders who asked if a straw was a simple machine. He opened a Google Doc and shared the link on Twitter, asking scientists and science educators to respond to his students. Over a few weeks, his students saw debate emerge in response to their simple machine question from scientists at the New York Hall of Science, a NASA astronaut, and physicists in the United Kingdom. High school teachers weighed in too. His students went from having one teacher to having many teachers including experts who took the time to share their thinking with his students (Thornton 2012).

When someone sees that others are taking risks, it can be an empowering moment of clarity. Beyond social media, it is time for teachers to explore more in their school and district. Classroom doors should be open, and administrators should challenge teachers to visit other classrooms. We think that all of us in education need to stop worrying about our mistakes and be open to criticism. In the end, this is about the students.

While this seems daunting given the pressures associated with current accountability systems, we know this can happen. However, making oneself vulnerable is easier said than done. It begins with seeking out like-minded peers who are willing to sit down with you—or even text with you—and talk about your professional successes and concerns.

To create a context for discussion, some schools are using what is called a pineapple chart to facilitate connectivity inside a school ("How Pineapple Charts Revolutionize Professional Development" 2016). The chart is placed in a visible area, and teachers can share on it in calendar format what they are doing and willing to open up to others to come see them at work.

We believe that administrators who support teachers with the time to view other classrooms within the school help develop a grassroots movement of change. Seeing is believing. Without witnessing risk and seeing its impact on student success, it can be difficult to understand why a change needs to happen.

Change involves an investment in the future. It is a process that will have its ups and downs. At times, changes lead to success, while other times, those changes will lead to failures. Both success and failure can be measured in different ways. But inevitably, there is knowledge to be learned from both. Failure is not the end. It is a step. Success is not the end. It is a step. Together learning cycles will always include successes and failures. Learning from both will help you move in the right direction to make changes that benefit learners.

When discussing change, motivation is another key element. There must be an intrinsic motivation to want to change. In order for that to happen, it is important for teachers to understand the value in changing. When you see the value in change, you will face challenges of making changes with more fervor. If you cannot find value or purpose in changing, the process will more than likely come to a stop.

This is where the vision of school becomes important. Administrators must promote professional growth and lifelong learning within the building. The administrator can demonstrate the importance of lifelong learning with the intention of influencing staff to seek more knowledge. For example, the principal who encourages teachers to form study groups around topics of interest from literacy strategies to project-based learning is investing in building the capacity of the school community.

Study groups can read a text together such as one on culturally responsive teaching and agree to practice strategies that they can bring back to the group to share. They can monitor results of their work, and the principal can provide faculty meeting time for teachers to lead a lesson on their work and action research with peers. The principal may share a blog that he or she follows with selected staff or a post he or she has written and even ask for feedback on it.

Anytime that teachers engage in conversation about their practices, it creates opportunities for questions and idea sharing. It also creates a path to lifelong learning. When school administrators sit at the table and participate in learning alongside teachers then ask to come in classes and practice strategies as a teacher, it accelerates and amplifies change while building credibility for the administrator as well.

Lifelong learning is an essential aspect of maturing as an individual and as a professional. There is always more to learn, and there is always room for growth. Educators should continuously seek ways to adapt their skills and improve in the classroom. Students deserve to be taught in a learning space where they have a model of lifelong learning leading the way. You can be that model.

Modeling lifelong learning increases the likelihood of it becoming a norm in your classroom. In addition, the more students who see lifelong learning in action, the more likely they will be to take risks as they learn. Sharing the work you do on your journey will help them as they travel along theirs.

YES...BUT

Making the decision to change is one thing, but the follow-through is another. Often there is a statement that prevents the follow through from happening. It is called the "yes ... but" statement. The statement might be in your own head, or it might come from a colleague. Either way, it should not stop the progress being made.

This is similar to deciding to go to the beach. You plan the trip, pack your bags, and drive all the way to the beach. Once there, you decide to not jump in the ocean because the water is too cold. You have done a lot of the work to plan the trip, and now it is time to enjoy the moment. Yes ... but at that last second, your thoughts convince you to not jump in. Even though you see a multitude of people enjoying the water, you decide to stay dry and sandy.

Don't let this be the case in the classroom. The purpose of seeing other learning spaces is to minimize your fear of failure. Yes, failure. It is a tough

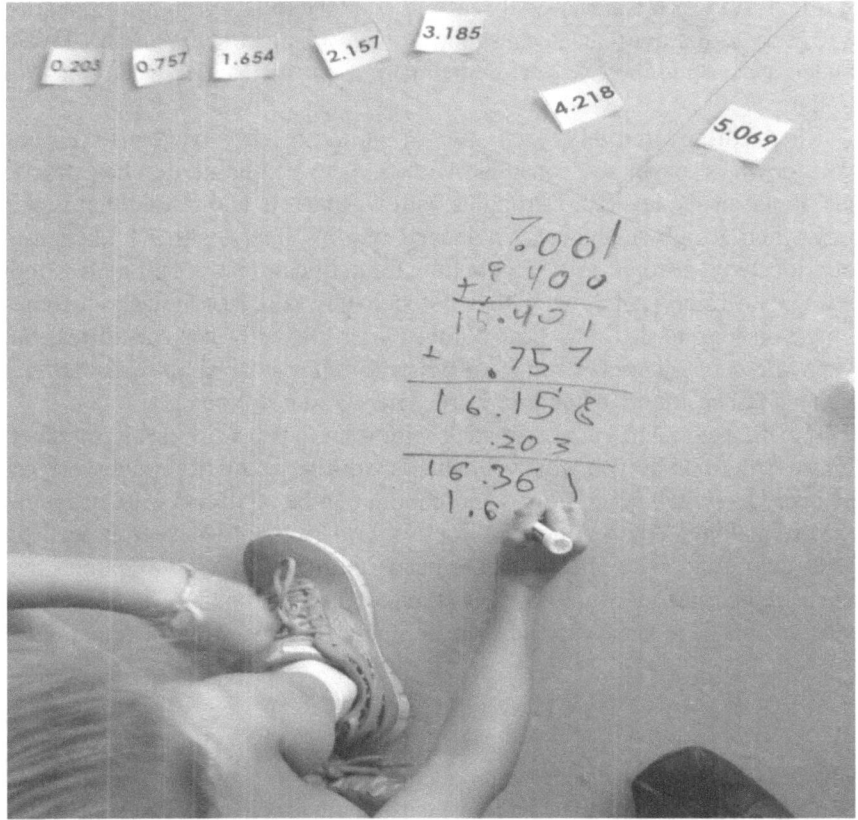

pill to swallow. It is a challenging foe, but one that will inevitably lead to learning. Failing is not preventable. It is going to happen. Shift your vision of failure so that you view it as a natural part of the learning process. Once you can truly see the importance of failure, your fear of it will diminish.

You can begin to take small risks after visiting other classrooms and analyzing your own strengths and weaknesses. After observing a peer, choose one aspect of your classroom or instructional practice that you would like to change. Yes, one small change is all that is needed to start. Think critically about what that one change should be. Allow your confidence to lead the way while you make the decision. You must have faith in your choice.

For example, if you are concerned about a student who is a struggling reader, then look for strategies to support that student. Find people who know something about reading strategies that you don't. The librarian may have ideas of new books that might jump-start or connect to the student's interests.

Learning from a peer how to more completely assess what a student's reading stumbling blocks are can lead you to a different strategy such as use of a text-to-speech app that will scaffold auditory inputs with print remarks. We've seen this over and over again in our own practice. We don't invent wheels very often, but we borrow them from our colleagues when our tires go flat.

Cheryl discovered this when after struggling to get a student to put one word down on paper she consulted with Ira who had come into her class to talk about his dyslexia and struggles with writing. He had shared that it was only when a high school teacher tapped into his interests that he began to laboriously type stories one letter at time for publication in his alt high school newspaper. Cheryl sat down with her student and said, "Tell me about something you love to do." His bear hunting wasn't exactly her cup of tea, but when she encouraged her reluctant writer to tell a story about bear hunting with his father, fourteen hundred words later he was still going.

If at first you don't succeed, stick with it and keep working. Remember, failure is defined by you. Analyze what is working and what is not working. Be ready to switch tasks around and continue to be confident in the changes you are making. When something doesn't work, it does not mean it needs to be thrown out. It just means that it needs more work. We've learned that when we put the work in, inevitably it makes learning better. That reinforces why we choose to teach especially those students who need us the most.

CHANGE IN ACTION

Meg is a kindergarten teacher and colleague. She has been teaching for more than thirty years. Over the last four years, she has reinvented herself in the classroom. Her space moved from being a more traditional kindergarten learning space to a space for risk.

She now presents at conferences, sharing her instructional practices with colleagues in our school communities and worldwide via Twitter, Facebook, Pinterest, and other social media platforms. She has become a model of risk taking. Her journey toward a space for risk began with a simple change in her classroom.

Meg decided a change should be made for her students to have a better learning experience. That is not to say that her previous students had a poor experience, but she knew there was room for growth. She has always been an excellent teacher. Her colleagues have relied on her words of wisdom for many years. But now, when her colleagues ask for wisdom, the advice she gives is much different than four years ago.

Her journey began by visiting and observing another kindergarten teacher's classroom. This particular teacher instructed using many nontraditional techniques, such as letting kindergartners sit on counters underneath windows to read or to stretch out on the floor to work on projects together. After visiting her colleague's classroom and discussing instructional decisions during team meetings, Meg decided it was time for a change.

As previously discussed, it is important to make one small change at a time. For her, that initial change was seating. She allowed her students to sit in more comfortable ways during instructional time. This simple change opened her eyes to much more. It allowed her to see that students could still focus on instruction even if they weren't all sitting in the same way.

She was able to take this new insight and apply it to other aspects of her instructional practices. Before long, Meg was designing lessons built around student engagement and student choice. She was giving them freedom in the classroom to make academic decisions—some of which led to failure. Her guidance and understanding allowed the students to see that failure was appropriate and natural.

JUMP ON IN, THE WATER IS FINE

At some point for educators, there needs to be a willingness to jump in. The students deserve the very best that can be offered. Can we truly say we are giving our best when something is left unchallenged that is holding some students back? Can educators truly devote their complete energy to each individual student when all options have not been explored? We are not perfect, and we work on these questions all the time.

These questions are not easily answered but should be analyzed. At the very least, every educator should feel confident in their individual progress as they move toward a more student-centered, risk-taking classroom environment. Students will not take risks in the classroom unless they know the room is ready for risk taking.

The flow of the space for students to take risks depends upon the leadership of the teacher. Children are very intuitive, and their instinctual decisions can be creatively inspiring when working in an environment that fosters that inspiration. Once started, the next step is to set up the classroom in a manner that pushes student creativity, collaboration, critical thinking, and risk.

We believe that learning occurs in real time for teachers. Whether it's a new technology application we heard about at lunch, a technology that will open a new learning pathway for students, or a strategy for setting up collaborative groups that we picked up in a Twitter chat when we open ourselves up to learning, we become a model for our students and peer teachers. As we move forward in our book, we invite you to consider, challenge, reflect, respond, and share what you are learning from our work.

WORKS CITED

"Doing Projects vs. Project Based Learning PBL." 2016. New Tech Network. August 8, 2016. https://newtechnetwork.org/resources/projects-vs-project-based-learning-pbl/.
Edutopia. 2015."Flexible Classrooms: Providing the Learning Environment That Kids Need." YouTube video, 4:18. August 3, 2015. https://www.youtube.com/watch?v=4cscJcRKYxA.
"How Pineapple Charts Revolutionize Professional Development." 2016. Cult of Pedagogy. September 25, 2016. https://www.cultofpedagogy.com/pineapple-charts/.
"Instructional Coaching." n.d. Albemarle County Public Schools. https://www2.k12albemarle.org/dept/instruction/instructional-coaching/Pages/default.aspx.
Thornton, Michael. 2012. "Is a Straw a Simple Machine?" Is a Straw a Simple Machine? Google Docs. https://docs.google.com/document/d/17cerqdkumZrtB5sXk4a4ezHIsOm87MyWVK3ww5tklK8/edit.

Chapter Three

Creating a Learning Space

The world is but a canvas to the imagination.—Henry David Thoreau

QUESTIONS TO PONDER IN THIS CHAPTER

- *How does a learning space dictate the type of learning that is happening in a classroom?*
- *How can teachers make adjustments to their current space to allow more risk to organically occur during the day?*
- *How can the space dictate the daily student-to-student and teacher-to-student interactions?*

THE CLASSROOM

The classroom is the central station of learning. Students must feel safe and comfortable in order for them to want to work as diligently as they can. By adapting current learning spaces to support choice and comfort for students, we have found that simple redesign of space can increase student attention to learning and decrease off-task behaviors. To reach the point where we made changes in our learning spaces, we had to step back and analyze ourselves. When we did, we found that we desire comfort in our own lives for proficient work to occur.

In this chapter, we will analyze the classroom and how you can adapt your current learning space to make it a student-centered classroom that fosters choice, comfort, and risk. K–8 teachers all over the country, indeed the world, are modifying classrooms to create more comfortable and innovative learning environments (Merrill 2017b). Changes in seating aren't limited to K–8 classrooms either. We also see grades 9–12 teachers in our district and beyond taking the risk to develop more choices for students in the arrangement of physical environment, regardless of class size, size of the classroom itself, or content area (Merrill 2017a).

A beneficial beginning would be to have your superintendent and administration on board regarding why having a space for risk is important for your students. Whether you have this support in the beginning is not crucial, but it is beneficial. You, as the classroom teacher, can create slight changes that make a profound impact upon your learning space. For example, simply enabling students to choose the location of their seat will lead to enhanced comfort.

The variety of seating in a class should vary because of differences in what students consider comfortable. When students can choose their location and what kind of seat is comfortable to them, they tell us they feel more at ease.

Furthermore, allowing students to occupy a choice of seating will inevitably lead them to value that they have more say in the classroom. This is a basic necessity for any space for risk and will help foster additional academic choice as well. We will discuss that in more depth later in this chapter.

HOW TO BEGIN?

Begin by developing a *choice and comfort student committee* within the classroom. Consider including students and their parents in the choice and comfort committee. Challenge them to become more attentive to spaces they observe outside the classroom. Ask them to be ready to share places they like with their friends.

Supply them with resources (such as an old cell phone or iPod that still has a working camera) to document the seating they prefer when they are at home, at a coffee shop, or in the local library. Be certain they understand the purpose of their task so that they are cognizant of the responsibility to represent their classroom peers to lead the classroom redesign process.

At the same time, document your own experiences. In addition, use websites and social media like Twitter, Instagram, or Pinterest to see what other teachers are implementing to alter their classrooms to augment choices that lead students to take learning risks. We've found great examples of how teachers use plastic bins of building and art materials to set up maker corners in their classrooms. In another case, we heard of a colleague who encouraged middle schoolers to write scripts for silent movies and then record videos to not just share with peers but to also broadcast to the world through a class YouTube account.

We believe that changing spaces just for the sake of changing space will not address the needs of learners. Instead, we've let our students guide us toward projects they would like to pursue, and in doing so we've had to make changes in our spaces to accommodate their interests and focus, from preparing a menu and cooking a meal for the entire class (math objectives) to 3D-printing artifacts that represent specific book scenes in novels students are reading.

Once your student committee is ready with their observations, collect their entire documentation and communicate that information to your class with focus on the similarities and differences in the seating. Begin to develop a seating layout for your space.

Money is an issue in all classrooms, so be certain to make this process as realistic as possible. The students might have a tremendous design for a different kind of learning space, so allow for that excitement, but also teach them that any decisions must represent fiscal responsibility.

Next consider asking the parent-teacher organization (PTO) or the school to utilize a portion of their funds to purchase a few pieces of furniture for your classroom. If that is not feasible, research and use websites like DonorsChoose to acquire a grant for your learning space. On Saturdays, go to as many yard sales as possible, and ask parents to do the same. Parents typically are gracious in donating former living room chairs, couches, and rugs. Start with what you can handle.

Witness the small successes in the room and allow that to motivate you, the students, and parents to initiate additional changes. See what works in the room and what doesn't. Every classroom is going to be different. For example, one teacher might begin by having a rug and several large pillows that allow students spaces to lounge or find a relaxing spot to read or collaborate with others to plan a project.

A teacher may discover that seventh-grade students do not prefer sitting on the floor. In that case, donate the pillows and the rug to a younger grade and shift to a variety of tables and seating. Altering the room to suit the students' needs is key, so this type of process should always point students to how their classroom needs to change to better serve them as learners.

WHAT IS NEXT? HOW DOES CHOICE IN SEATING TRANSFER TO MORE ACADEMIC CHOICES?

We usually begin the year by conducting "getting acquainted activities," along with our usual icebreakers. Learning students' names, strengths, weaknesses, and interests at any age is key to building the trust and respect that will sustain both you and your students through life. When students walk into our classrooms, they realize that it is not a traditional desks-and-chairs-in-rows classroom. Our students can take advantage of the options we offer them, and we can craft choices that will be of interest to individual students;

we begin the year by mapping as much background as we can on each student in our classes.

Developing a confidential record on each student helps to map personal and academic strengths and growth opportunities. We consider those as we work to teach situationally with the goals of each student in mind. If students understand our commitment to them, they will open up to us, and to other students in the class, about pertinent personal situations, therefore making connections that help us gain insight into who they are as learners, socioemotionally and academically.

Knowing what leads students to do their best work and feel safe in class is key to building relationships and reinforcing the connections that students have with their fellow classmates and you. Once you acquire additional knowledge of the students, and what makes them tick (or not), they can continue the movement forward, with their best interests in mind.

In the classroom—whether it is seating, purchasing supplies, specific lessons, or even learning how to make choices—your students' interests, strengths, and challenges are always kept in the front of every decision. The students are the teacher's purpose for being there. Welcome them to *their* room!

Ask students to develop, create, and apply ideas for the bulletin boards and walls. After all, you are not the center of the classroom, the students are. Let the students own and take charge of their learning. When students feel comfortable enough in the classroom, they will soar to their highest peak of achievement.

START SMALL

Trying to implement numerous changes in the classroom at one time can be detrimental to the process. Add a few items at a time and ensure that it is beneficial to the learning space. Continue to add what the committee suggests and thinks is advantageous for the students' space to allow for risk.

An effortless method to activate enabling additional choice in the classroom is when students are able to choose the members of their group. It might not be the teacher's choice of who would work best together, but allow the students to figure this out through trial and error. Mandate objectives, goals, or learning targets; discuss the topic, including students' input; and have them choose between multiple activities they'd like to integrate to sharpen that concept.

As long as a goal is still being met, students should have choices of how to learn the material. Once students complete that task, reflect with students as a class or individually. Consider asking questions about their choice to work alone or collaboratively. "How did that work for you choosing your

Creating a Learning Space

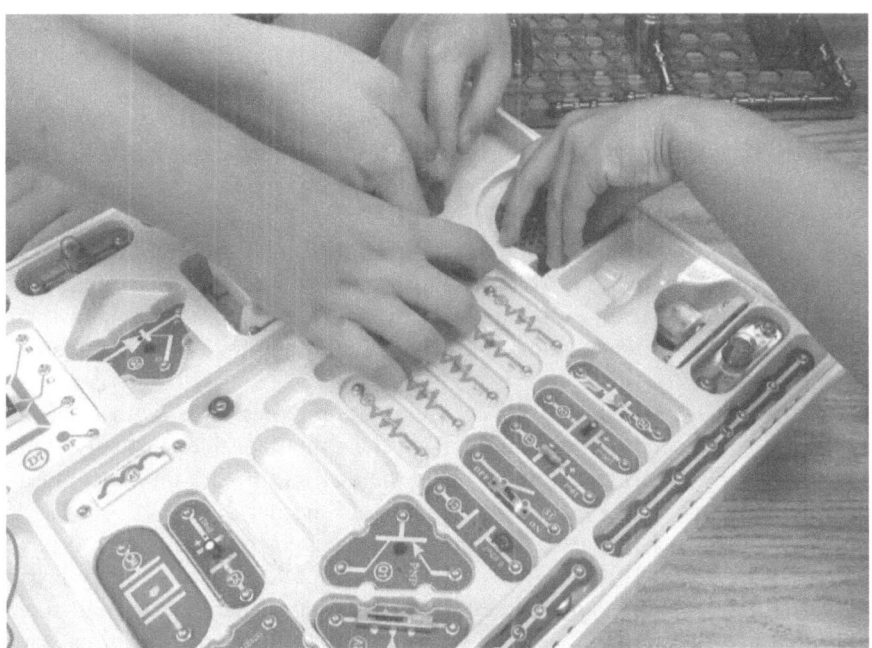

partner?" "Reflect upon strategies you used to work with your partner. How did those work?" "Would you choose the same partner next time? Why or why not?" This helps students to begin to think metacognitively across academic and social spheres (Owen and Vista 2017).

When you think students are ready to expand the range of choices in their work, allow them to choose a group of two, three, or four to conduct the project. Next, identify your expectations and deadlines for completing work. When ready, support students as they commence planning. Do students plan on their phones? Tablets? Laptops? Paper? It is the students' choice with whom they work and how they plan.

However, this is not an "anything goes" moment. Be sure that you have communicated both to the class and to individuals who need more up-close-and-personal time with you what your expectations are for project work, tool use, and collaboration. Involve them in helping to define and shape the class norms for project work.

After you set the framework for the students' first project, students will plan and map out what needs to be completed and by when. The teacher is the "guide on the side," the facilitator who moves the process along. The teacher walks and sits near groups to hear ideas and ask probing higher-order-thinking questions.

We see several important question stems as key to teams getting started: "Why is _____ important or significant to your project? What other ideas about _____ have you considered? How might you connect those ideas together? Which details or information is most important here and why? What do you think is so interesting about your project that will make others intrigued or want to know more?" Students discuss these questions in their groups, reflect, and move forward to deciding which medium best fits for this particular project.

Holding the students accountable for their decisions and monitoring who is meeting each deadline is an essential role for you as well as members of the group. Student teams also must identify the audience with whom they want to share their presentation and why. Should they invite other students/ teachers? Parents?

Will this be a series of stand-up presentations, or a class exposition, or showcase for projects? How might they share their project virtually with peers in other schools inside and outside the district through online communication tools such as Skype, Zoom, or Google Hangouts?

Would they like to construct a project web page or make a video to post online? What tech skills and tools will they need, and how might they learn those? If they see their authentic audience as being outside the school, such as with a presentation to the school board or a community organization, how will they make contact to schedule that?

You as the teacher will need to help some student teams more than others think about their final project presentation and what audience and presentation format will best suit their needs. In your facilitator role, by asking more questions and giving less direction, students will begin to own the project and realize you really mean that they need to be in charge of the project, not you.

When completing a project, rubrics can be used as a guide for students. However, teachers should be wary of *always* relying on teacher-built rubrics. If not constructed thoughtfully, rubrics can hinder the creative process and also limit the amount of risk taking. If a rubric is to be used, have the students create it. You can share a variety of rubrics on websites with the whole class to help them choose one that makes sense for their project, or they can choose to create their own using examples you have shared.

We have a colleague who came up with a unique strategy for scaffolding students into building their own rubric. On a one-to-four-scaled rubric, he would add the descriptive details for two and three on the scale, but ask the students to do that for four and one. He would label the "four" category as the "wow" factor and the "one" category as "not yet." The students would fill in a description of what their "wow" factor would be as well as their "not yet." Another strategy we've found to help students get started is to pick a common task that students may do, such a making a sandwich or riding a skateboard, and ask them to design a rubric for different levels of success in

accomplishing those tasks: one = not yet, two = developing, three = competent, four = advanced/wow!

Students are much harder on themselves than teachers usually are on them. As you circulate around the room, you should be listening to teams and asking how they are all participating to complete their project tasks and doing their "fair share."

It can be a challenge with choice-driven academic projects when some students seem to be pulling more of the weight of the projects than others. Your role as facilitator again is critically important in helping students to learn the skills of working collaboratively, especially since the most common group project complaint we've heard over the years is "He/she isn't doing their part." (This isn't just relevant to student teams—we've heard it on teacher teams too.)

This is not easily remedied, but can be worked out. You must be proactive when facilitating this creative process. If this situation arises, a whole-group or small-group discussion is warranted. Work with the students and build a working agreement to dictate better results. This can happen by taking a project time-out with a team and scheduling a time to miniconference with them. Using your whole-class meeting problem-solving format with the small group (Bafile 2016):

1. Ask each team member to describe the problem and why it's a problem without blaming another student in a negative way. This is a critical skill. You might say, "I needed to team plan with a colleague, and I really didn't want to spend the time doing it. That's when my teaching partner came to me and said that we need to talk because she couldn't do the work by herself—and it wasn't fair. That's when I had to think about how my choice was affecting her and what I needed to do." You could ask them to write this down individually, but having them get used to sharing problems aloud is a great skill for life.
2. Ask each team member to describe what they can do to help solve the problems they believe are keeping the team from working together successfully. List those so everyone in the team can see.
3. Work with the team to come up with strategies to make the solution work. These could be as simple as setting a cell phone timer for getting everyone started on the work or even changing a project assignment if one team member is struggling with his or her assignment. They might even find a business project management tool online they like and want to use. They also might ask if you can check in with them more often until they get on track.
4. After the team decides how they will proceed, ask them to write down the problem they are solving and the solutions on a work contract, and have them sign it (and you sign it as well).

Learning to do projects together is an imperfect process for students and one that takes your commitment to coaching, mentoring, guiding, supervising, and even occasionally offering more direction to some teams than others. Remember that students don't learn project team skills typically in their homes and these don't come naturally. It's why teachers are incredibly important beyond the high-tech tools our students get to use today. We don't think we can be replaced with robots because we teach!

Whenever students create or make something, as we discussed earlier, they should be given the opportunity to share their work with their peers, teacher, parents, and even the world. Twitter, Facebook, LiveBinders, and other social media enable students to connect and share their progress and hard work with people all over the world ("Five Ways to Use Technology and Digital Media for Global Learning," n.d.).

For students to have a range of audiences for their work, you will need to give students the opportunity and time to share. When presenting their work, figuring out how the audience can give feedback, even virtually, also is a consideration. For the presentation to be interactive and meaningful to the audience and the presenters, the audience will need the chance to ask questions and offer positive feedback and constructive criticism, either virtually, on paper, or aloud.

The learning space is a pivotal piece of the puzzle. As with adults, children need comfort when they work. Comfort can be provided in many ways. The space itself must be welcoming and include spaces that enable students to kick back, relax, and learn with physical comfort.

Emotional comfort can be created through many avenues, but giving students more academic choice in the learning space will help facilitate this process. Students revel in choice. They take ownership of creating projects/products. They take ownership of their learning in spaces for risk. This will be discussed in more depth in chapters 11 and 12.

WORKS CITED

Bafile, Cara. 2016. "Class Meetings: A Democratic Approach to Classroom Management." Education World. Last updated November 11, 2016. https://www.educationworld.com/a_curr/profdev/profdev012.shtml.

"Five Ways to Use Technology and Digital Media for Global Learning." n.d. Asia Society. Accessed July 8, 2018. https://asiasociety.org/education/five-ways-use-technology-and-digital-media-global-learning.

Merrill, Stephen. 2017a. "High School Flexible Seating Done Right." Edutopia. George Lucas Educational Foundation. August 8, 2017. https://www.edutopia.org/article/high-school-flexible-seating-done-right.

———. 2017b. "7 Outstanding K–8 Flexible Classrooms." Edutopia. George Lucas Educational Foundation. September 8, 2017. https://www.edutopia.org/article/7-outstanding-k-8-flexible-classrooms.

Owen, David, and Alvin Vista. 2017. "Strategies for Teaching Metacognition in Classrooms." Brookings. November 15, 2017. https://www.brookings.edu/blog/education-plus-development/2017/11/15/strategies-for-teaching-metacognition-in-classrooms/.

Chapter Four

Teacher Autonomy

Control leads to compliance, autonomy leads to engagement.—Daniel Pink

QUESTIONS TO PONDER IN THIS CHAPTER

- *What is teacher autonomy? Why is it important?*
- *How can teachers create an autonomous environment in their classroom?*
- *What can stand in the way of teacher autonomy?*
- *Once a teacher has an autonomous classroom, how will it help build a space for risk?*

WHAT IS TEACHER AUTONOMY?

Understanding the importance of teacher autonomy means also having a clear understanding of what autonomy means in the context of working for organizations, in our case schools. Autonomy begins with a sense of efficacy and trust and can be defined as "the power to shape your work environment in ways that allow you to perform at your best." It does not mean "doing whatever you like, working in isolation, or working without a net" (Maylett 2016).

We can't emphasize enough that it's essential to visit other classroom teachers who have created flexible, collaborative environments that allow learners to have choices of a variety of spaces from quiet, individual spaces to more open collaborative spaces—indeed what sometimes are referred to as caves, campfires, and watering holes. We have to confirm the belief that when our young people have opportunities to make their own learning choices, whether it's where a learner chooses to work in class or a team makes a decision about what option for a project they choose to pursue, watching other professionals helps prove that when we give students choice, we free them to learn and we shift power from the teacher to the learners.

This is essential to developing both physical and emotional space for taking learning risks. In fact, it is an important step to understanding why a space for risk is beneficial for learners and teachers.

A collaborative culture is not just important, indeed we believe it is essential in a space for risk. While supporting development of a collaborative culture is an autonomous choice that you can exercise independent of others in your building, we believe it limits possibilities when teachers lack a peer network. No one should feel alone in one's efforts to shift practices, which is why we purposely seek out other educators so that we are part of a professional learning community (PLC). Our participation in a professional learning community builds a support system that empowers us, that pushes us forward (DuFour, DuFour, and Eaker 2008).

Why do teachers need autonomy? Autonomy provides teachers space to make critical decisions in the classroom and in the best of school cultures is supported by administrators and peers. Affording autonomy to teachers represents a relationship of trust and professional regard between the administration and teachers in a school. In this chapter, the teacher's role in this relationship will be discussed and analyzed. The administrator's role will be discussed in more detail in the second part of this book.

Building principals have countless responsibilities within a school. One such responsibility is working with stakeholders to create a school mission statement. For example, at Cheryl's middle school, the following mission statement guides learning there: "Sutherland Middle School believes that striving for creative excellence today prepares students to succeed in the changing and challenging world tomorrow" ("SMS Fact Sheet," n.d.).

If a mission statement, however, is simply words on a page and what occurs in the classrooms of a school doesn't align to the mission, then it sets the stage for a school staff who "talk the talk" but who do not "walk the mission walk." Administrators in a school must work with stakeholders to align, clearly articulate, and engage staff in developing contextual and conceptual understanding of what the mission means as it defines the learning culture of the school. It is the responsibility of all of us to execute this mission within the environment of our classrooms.

In Cheryl's school, this looks like a project-based learning focus that involves students in work that has a community impact, whether it is a science class working on 3D-printing prosthetic hands to donate to an international organization or researching the World War II Holocaust in a language arts class and building a memorial outdoors in a school garden area. When you align the design of learning plans for your students, with your school's mission, you stay true to the goals of the school. This congruency between the established mission and the work that your students are doing leads to trust from administrators in your autonomy as a teacher.

After the principal has clearly articulated with stakeholders and staff the agreed upon mission, the opportunity for you, and team members, to make decisions about how to support learners to meet established outcomes makes sense to administrators and teachers alike—not in isolation from each other but in partnership through professional learning community structures and coteaching and coherent with the school's mission. We suggest that you revisit your mission and consider what it means as you consider the learning experiences that you create for students.

While administrators handle the day-to-day responsibilities of running a learning institution, the critical work of teachers in their classrooms makes sure the school's mission comes to fruition. To advantage students to the greatest degree possible, administrators and teachers must work together functionally. When this happens, everyone benefits.

Open communication occurs with clarity and honesty. Collective efficacy becomes normative because everyone pitches in to support the mission work. Peers share resources and ideas to help with challenges. In schools where the mission statement and mission actions align, teachers look for opportunities to collaborate to help a colleague. This could mean taking the risk to mentor or tutor a student who is not in your classroom or even grade level.

In Michael's former school, teachers committed to quarterly open mini-expositions of project work so that students could see the work of older and younger students as well as do short presentations of their projects. This was consistent with both the school's mission and objectives for learning: "We are committed to empowering all students to be creative lifelong learners and productive global citizens through relationships, compassion and perseverance" ("About Agnor-Hurt Elementary School," n.d.).

To accomplish this mission, staff came to consensus on a school-wide objective that every student would have a project on display in a project-based learning museum to showcase their critical and creative thinking as well as their ability to collaborate. They considered that most projects made at school and on display would likely not be perfect.

The staff had a specific rationale for all students completing projects at school. First, they allowed students to collaborate with peers. Second, staff also knew that students who created projects from scratch at school rather than "parent-supported" projects at home would not necessarily have polished work on display. The teachers decided, however, that this work was far more representative of students' independent work than that completed at home for several reasons.

Children from middle-class homes often have projects that have been resourced and polished with parent support. Children from families lacking financial means often experience the inequity of resources and support in

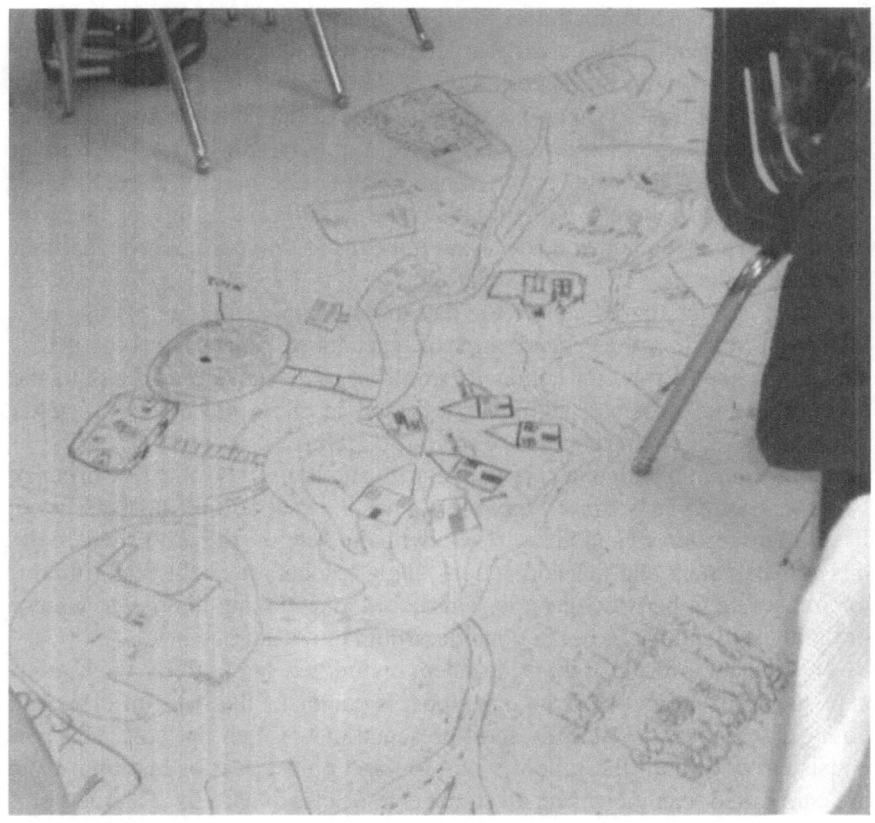

their homes. To ensure that the equity-driven mission of Michael's former school aligned with the work that the children accomplished, teachers decided that all projects would be completed at school.

Teacher autonomy becomes crucial when negotiating collaborative work with peers. No teacher should be an island. But teachers do need enough space to make critical decisions in the classroom without feeling as though their every step is being critiqued. If or when teachers feel micromanaged, their teaching can suffer. In turn, students will learn less and the mission and vision of the school will falter from lack of alignment.

WHY AUTONOMY?

The classroom is an ever-evolving space for learning. Yesterday is different than today, and today will be different than tomorrow. The twenty-first-century student is undoubtedly different. Educators must respect and respond to those differences without judgment. To do so, teachers should develop a new vision for their classroom. This involves challenging traditional approaches and trying new instructional techniques.

A few years ago, one of our peers who has been teaching for a number of years in a traditional elementary school began to question whether the practices she was using allowed students to integrate new tools into their work. She had been learning from a peer about how to use social media as teaching tools as well as for networking with professionals.

Soon, not only was she on Twitter, but she also was involving her students in using a variety of apps including social media apps. One of the outcomes of her work with students was construction of an "apps" alphabet to hang in her class. Her class went from paper-pencil dependent to using laptops and tablet devices to access a world of information as well as to create blogs, tweets, and videos to share with others.

Autonomy in teaching is not always easy. We've found that we can't be autonomous and fear failing. To have failures become a part of the adult learning cycle, opportunities for administrators and teachers to work together to learn from both successes and the failures in the classroom have to be incorporated into instructional coaching sessions, PLCs, staff meetings, and teacher-principal conferences.

If teachers feel overly supervised, fear can lead them to continually question their decisions in the classroom. We have to be responsible for what occurs in our classes, but there must also be freedom to fail, succeed, and ultimately learn without fear of life-altering consequences.

How can teachers build a level of autonomy in their classroom without being disconnected from colleagues and the principal? First, each teacher should meet early in the year with their supervisor to discuss expectations. Both the supervisor and the teacher should be specific regarding what they expect of each other in a school culture that encourages risk, collaboration, and autonomy. A positive working relationship between the teachers and administrator is nonnegotiable.

We've identified seven basics of interaction among staff and the principal to guide a school community toward a culture that values autonomy, democratic learning, and continuous growth:

1. Demonstrate honesty in giving and receiving feedback to each other.
2. Be kind in your honesty as you share the bright spots of the work being accomplished as well as areas for improvement.
3. Realize that autonomy means that teachers are afforded the time to shape their classroom environment based on the needs of students in the classroom—with the caveat that autonomy also means that student work must align with the mission.

4. Open communication is critical and should occur often, transparently and consistently so there are no surprises for either the teacher or the principal.
5. Areas of freedom and autonomy are identified and agreed upon together.
6. A protocol is used when conflict emerges to find a mutually agreeable solution if at all possible.
7. The needs of children come before adults—always.

Identifying and discussing expectations for each other is not always an easy conversation, but it is an important one to set goals that are mutually acceptable and with an assumption that you will have a high degree of autonomy in your classroom.

Often this beginning-of-the-year discussion is teacher centered even if the administrator leads the flow of the conversation. In what is often your goal-setting discussion, consider writing down ahead of time the points to assert as critical to you and that give voice to your desires for the school year. Also, you should be specific about the challenges you want to face and overcome. Furthermore, during this initial meeting, this is when you should be ready to outline your plan of action that you will advocate for implementing. This involves three stages in your process of engaging with the principal:

1. Specifically outline any proposed physical adaptations to the learning space and any intended instructional changes such as a shift to using project-based learning and setting up a creation station as a makerspace. A plan of action should be unique to you—given your specific learning space and students. Regardless, this is a very important step.
2. Identify the intentional outcomes that you expect to result from your shifts in space and practice and how you will know. You might identify increased engagement that leads to acquisition of more complex communication competencies. How will you know? This could come in assessment of portfolios, rubrics on a performance task, or decontextualized assessments that are used in your school. The sooner the principal understands and supports your intentions for the year, the sooner an agreement can be solidified that reflects your autonomy in making changes in your classroom.
3. Invite your principal to observe your classroom as early as possible in the school year. Let it be known that the door is always open to peers as well. Openly ask for critiques about the space and the instructional practices observed. This journey cannot and should not be taken alone. Your administrator is an important ally as changes are being made to the learning space and instruction.

STAND OUT, STAND TALL, STAND STRONG

Anything that is worth changing takes work and perseverance. Creating a space for risk will not be easy. There will be pitfalls. There will be days that are harder than others. But there will also be wonderful moments, and those moments will begin to compound into a grassroots movement of change in the classroom.

Along the way, there might be people who stand in the way. The key reason it's vitally important to meet with your supervising administrator early in the year to discuss a plan of action is to make sure that you both are on the same page. When you are not seeing the same vision, difficulties can arise. As an educator, the number one goal we all should hold is to see every student succeed. Unfortunately, there are instances in which egos and personalities stand in the way of that goal.

If your supervising administrator isn't aligned with your vision for creating a space for risk for your students—and you—it will be hard to have an autonomous learning space. Having autonomy is built from the faith developed between an administrator and his or her staff. Even though this will be a challenge, it does not have to be the end of the journey. Remember, the students are worth the fight.

We haven't always had the full support of principals for some of the changes we've made. Sometimes administrators have been skeptical but willing to let us move forward. Other times, they've been quite resistant; but more often with a good rationale in front of them, they have been willing for us to be the explorers who venture into new territory before others follow.

Transparency is key to autonomy. An open-door policy will help administrators feel more informed about the changes you are making. Always be prepared to explain why you are taking a certain action. When the principal does observe, remember to be as specific as possible in describing what the principal is seeing. We've found over the years when people observe our classes, they may make inferences based on prior assumptions about what an engaged class looks like. In some cases, their perspective is more informed by compliance-driven culture than engagement culture.

You will need to help them observe, talk with students, and see ongoing work in progress so that they understand that an engaged classroom is noisier than a compliance-driven one because collaboration is the norm for active learners. Learners have permission to get up and move to get the tools and supplies they need and to choose to work on the floor, sit, or stand as they work.

Students who are active learners experience class differently, because they can pursue choice and comfort on their own terms as long as they are respecting community. When possible, meet with the administration before a planned observation so you can discuss what they will see and how they can interface with students to get perspective. Always reiterate your interest in hearing about bright spots they observe as well as feedback and questions on any areas that aren't where you want them to be yet.

In a planned observation, lesson objectives should be thoroughly developed and passed along to administrators so that they have a clear indication of what they will see that matches agreed upon "look-fors." Having said that, creativity cannot be fully articulated in a lesson plan, so leave time within the plan's implementation for student ingenuity, spontaneity, and creative choice. It is those special, creative student moments that will help an unconvinced administrator begin to understand the power of a space for risk.

Your openness to a student's ideas for a project that is going in a different direction than anticipated models the same for the principal. When a student team comes over to you to say they've decided to make a video to share with the superintendent about wasted food in the cafeteria rather than simply write a letter as they had planned, this demonstrates that you are open to students using new tools for communication.

Communicate with the administrator certain aspects of the lesson for which you would value feedback. Giving administrators specific targets will help them focus their observation. It will also allow you to highlight certain steps in the lesson. For example, we have highlighted the aspects of the

---

Dear Mr. Thornton,   June 4, 20

    Respect is the one rule we were told to abide by, and in my opinion, one of the most valuable lessons in life. You taught me to think and question and to challenge what isn't right. Some things that I learned weren't in curriculum, (actually, most weren't) but I gained more than I ever could have from only what you were told to teach. You challenged me, and inspired too. I perceive the world differently and attribute it to you. Also this year, I watched my peers grow and develop and become caring compassionate people under your gaze. You taught to break barriers and surpass expectations. You taught us like who we are- *innovators to the future of tomorrow*. Each one of us is going to be the change, make a change, and there is nothing more precious than encouraging and promoting that.

    Thank you so much for everything you do for each and everyone of us.

lesson that demonstrate student creativity, student choice, and peer collaboration to match an engagement goal that we have both set in past years.

Once the school year has begun, it becomes harder and harder to find time to meet face-to-face with the principal. Nonetheless, it is imperative that there is a postobservation meeting even if it is only for fifteen minutes. In this meeting, honesty is paramount. You must be honest about your approach and why the activity transpired in the manner that it did and also be ready to discuss any failures that occurred.

The principal should highlight what the principal perceived worked or didn't work from his or her observation, and also be honest about the overall perception of the classroom. This dialogue will lead to professional growth for both the administrator and you. Remember, when you leave the door open to the classroom and continue to invite administrators into the learning space, they will be more likely to drop in and get to know the learners in your classroom as well as you.

By sharing stories of success with the principal, it will motivate him or her to observe more often. This can be just a quick hallway chat, a handwritten invite from students to an upcoming presentation, a link to a private video of the class at work, or a brief email sound bite about something that has occurred. Again, your ultimate goal is to develop a relationship of trust that enables you the freedom to work in a space of risk without feeling pressure to not make mistakes and possibly fail.

AUTONOMY AND A SPACE FOR RISK

After establishing an autonomous space, it's time to evaluate the classroom. This must be a genuine evaluation to audit how instruction, furniture, space, and planning changes are functioning. Before you are ready for this, you must have a sincere openness to adapting classroom space that is informed by student input and your own goal to increase opportunities for creativity and choice.

Often the classroom is viewed as a space where students and you as teacher are separated because of authority. However, some teachers tend to view the classroom as theirs so the decision-making rests solely in their hands. Before you begin to involve students in designing the learning spaces they need, we recommend you take the time to assess and reflect upon your own tolerance for ambiguity. After all, nothing challenges our sense of order as educators like kids rearranging a classroom. Some teachers have totally freed students.

We remember the very experienced fifth-grade teaching peer who piled everything stored in the class on desks all stacked in the center of the room and shared that it was *their* (students') room to arrange to meet *their* needs.

In a follow-up conversation later in the year, he said that he'd had fewer questions about where resources were located than in any year prior to doing this. For another peer, simply supporting students to move desks into groups for collaboration was her first step to more active and engaged learning.

However, if you fear involving students as decision makers about their space, we encourage you to dive more deeply into your philosophy about classroom control. After all, if you've been granted autonomy by the principal, it's time to pass along that autonomy to the students as well. The learning space should be viewed as ours, not yours or mine. The students need to have ownership of the space. It is a mutual relationship grounded in meeting the needs of the community.

Let the students have a voice about furniture and the arrangement of the room. Give them ample time to critically think about what it is they need to be successful. Analyze their perspectives and together agree upon some realistic changes that can be made to the learning space. For example, consider this dialogue:

Students: We would really like to have a reading bike in the corner of the class.

Teacher: Hmmm, that's interesting. How would that help you?

Students: We see people reading on exercise bikes on TV and Caitlin says her mother does it all the time. Some of us need to move a lot rather than just sit still. This might help.

Teacher: I like this idea, but I'm not sure where we could get an exercise bike.

Students: Let's ask the parents or see if we can find someone to donate one.

Teacher: What a great way to avoid having to buy one. Who would like to write a letter to the principal and PTO to see if we can get their support and help?

Students: YES!!!

The teacher and the students should also discuss instructional planning and design. This will lead to more investment by the students, which will help build a positive relationship in the classroom. These are not easy steps to make, but ones that will help build a positive, risk-taking learning environment.

Student suggestions, student criticisms are essential. Some are more realistic than others, but every student thought has value to you, telling you how your work, your environment, and your presentations are perceived. Students who understand their role in the process will believe in the direction of the class.

The freedom that the teacher feels will foster more creativity while developing lessons. It will also promote less fear of failure. The students need to feel these same things so that the space is truly ready for risk taking. Once both parties have a sense of freedom and autonomy, real creativity can blossom. This, of course, will lead to some failures. That is good. Failing is inevitably part of learning.

None of these changes will be easy at first. They involve a deep, passionate desire to do something different, a dedication to creating a learning environment that is different and more student centered. A growth mind-set is important for every teacher. Your own change process relies on you to be determined to never be satisfied with your progress.

Each day is a new day of learning. When you experience autonomy as a teacher, you become freer to experiment with strategies that will help all students to find success in your class. In exercising your autonomy and even sharing what changes you are making and why with your students, you become a model for lifelong learning alongside your learners.

WORKS CITED

"About Agnor-Hurt Elementary School." n d. Albemarle County Public Schools. Accessed July 8, 2018. https://www2.k12albemarle.org/school/AHES/about/Pages/default.aspx.

DuFour, Richard, Rebecca DuFour, and Robert Eaker. 2008. *Revisiting Professional Learning Communities at Work: New Insights for Improving Schools*. Bloomington, IN: Solution Tree.

Maylett, Tracy. 2016. "6 Ways to Encourage Autonomy with Your Employees." Entrepreneur. March 4, 2016. https://www.entrepreneur.com/article/254030.

"SMS Fact Sheet." n.d. Albemarle County Public Schools. Accessed July 8, 2018. https //www2.k12albemarle.org/school/SMS/about/Pages/fact-sheet.aspx.

Chapter Five

Growth Mind-Set

Sometimes when you innovate, you make mistakes. It is best to admit them quickly, and get on with improving your other innovations.—Steve Jobs

QUESTIONS TO PONDER IN THIS CHAPTER

- *Are the students taking responsibility in learning how to learn to assist them in preparing for the working world?*
- *Do the work areas, for the students, allow them to be innovative and produce their best work?*
- *Is the teacher well versed in the most recent research of what's best for students?*

BUILDING A UNIFIED MIND-SET

We are all in this together: students, parents, administrators, and teachers. The culture of a classroom, of a school, is either a community of learners, or it is a place devoted to compliance. Compliance is not learning for one's life, but rather on someone's agenda.

Learning spaces either include the tools, the rhythms, the culture of the community of students, or they are simply classrooms designed to limit which students get to succeed or not.

There is a mind-set in the classroom that's apparent when the teacher and students are all in learning the work together. When you visit the classroom, the feeling is palpable that this is *our* classroom and these are *our* technologies, books, and creation resources to utilize, to research, and to further our learning. Students simply pick up and use their iPhone, tablet, laptop, iPod, et cetera for learning purposes.

If there is a YouTube example, the teacher happily shows it on the screen or whiteboard, or the students each can see it on their device of choice (DOC). Having a bring your own device (BYOD) mind-set is important in the twenty-first-century classroom, and in Cheryl's class that means students having a choice of technology tools—some of which are traditional technology such as books, pens, or paintbrushes, and some are current technologies such as a 3D printer or a cell phone.

We attempt to model new concepts we are introducing in content areas using a variety of technologies, including numerous manipulatives. There are a variety of learning preferences demonstrated by students in the classroom, and each needs to be addressed each and every day. How does the teacher do this?

For example, you will see references throughout chapters in this book to how teachers use notebooks, virtual documents, or a typical composition book to list each child's strengths, areas for growth, and interests. Only the teacher can view this because information about a student's IEP (Individualized Education Program), 504 plan, student and parent requests, and the teacher's individual accommodations are listed in this notebook. This confidential journal is either in the teacher's hand or under lock and key at all times.

As you plan a lesson, the needs of students are kept in mind and are followed with intentional focus on a daily basis. For example, you can demonstrate, utilizing interactive technologies, how to address different preferences for learning inputs in a variety of ways.

You might engage learners using YouTube or United Streaming videos or through interesting online articles that you have curated as reading options. Using multiple teaching techniques to deepen learning helps to create a context of relevancy to the content students are learning. Here are a few specific examples of strategies we use:

- Expert groups make sense when you want students to cogenerate learning across the entire class. You can take a specific event in history such as the American Revolution and ask each group to research a different point of view about it: Tory families, Patriot families, King George II, and Thomas Jefferson. After researching the event and creating points-of-view information, each member of the group reconvenes in a new group and teaches the point of view that their group developed (Tallman 2014).
- Numbered heads together works well when you want to develop diverse teams in terms of skill levels. After you assign students into teams, students number off from one to four. You can then pose a question, provide wait time for the group to land on an answer, and then ask for students with a specific number (all the fours, for example) to respond. You can then follow through by asking all the number threes to share whether they

agree or disagree. This is a great way to get teams to analyze inferred meaning in a reading passage, for math problems, or to give a relevant example of a science concept ("Improve Group Responding: Numbered Heads Together," n.d.).
- Nonlinguistic representations are documented as critical for students to process language-based descriptions of concepts they are learning. While you can create nonlinguistic representations (an excellent universal design for learning strategy), anytime that you can have students create their own nonlinguistic representations, they are more likely to transfer the concept into long-term memory. These are exemplified through showing class survey data in a Venn diagram or a flowchart that visually illustrates the steps of a science experiment procedure (Marzano 2010).
- Metacognitive strategies help students reflect upon how they think about solving problems, what they are reading, or what steps they might take to complete an assignment. Think-pair-share when students partner and take turns listening to each other describe their thinking. When a student talks through with a partner what strategy they used and why to solve a math problem, they are exercising metacognition, which John Hattie labels as having significant effect size on learning in his research ("Ten Metacognitive Teaching Strategies," n.d.).

When a teacher uses a maker-infused curriculum, it is helpful to learners to see a model of several examples. The teacher can write examples generated by the class on the whiteboard or type them into the computer and show on a projector screen. Inquiry learning and project-, problem-, and passion-based learning can all be utilized as paths that can incorporate maker work into the work of students. When students make the components they need in a project that captures their interests to contextualize content, they are engaged constantly and consistently.

Most students need to see, hear, and activate information a few times before it travels as knowledge and/or skills from short-term memory to long-term memory. This is where multiple strategies help solidify deeper learning among all students, not just the very few who can hear something once and recall it immediately. Once you have introduced new material and/or concepts to students, they need to begin delving into the topic in a deeper sense, not through repetition. This is why using the new Bloom's or SOLO taxonomies as a frame for how to deepen learning is a key in your planning. If you don't do this now, researching and using the taxonomies can be a growth challenge that's worth pursuing.

Chapter 5

CLASS STRATEGIES

Sometime, near the beginning of the year, you should talk with both parents and students to explain that each student learns at a different pace. If you feel (or your learners feel) that they need to move onward into differentiated opportunities, they may do so. You usually know who will need to do this from a preassessment of the material that can be as informal as a KWL (already know, want to know, have learned) discussion at the beginning of a unit.

If a student already knows the material or concepts you are about to teach, why would the student need to "relearn" them? Students have the right to learn at their own pace. It is not difficult, after an assessment—which includes vocabulary and concepts—for a student to move forward at his or her own pace. For example, if you are introducing the concept of the power of setting to shape a novel, and a student already has a clear understanding of that, the student might decide to write a short story utilizing the concept of setting.

Cheryl has used upper levels of Bloom's higher-level-thinking taxonomy to engage students in creating artifacts represented as critically important to a novel's story-line or characters. She has had students create a 2D image of an artifact using a program called "Design 1, 2, 3." Students then print it on the 3D printer. Students have moved from these 2D images they have created on-screen to a 3D-printed artifact that stimulates their creativity to write an amazing story, make a scrapbook, or turn printed objects into a game board that tells a story. After prompts from Cheryl, at the beginning of the year, each student knows when it is okay to branch off along their own learning paths to delve into what interests them. *They* take charge of *their* learning.

When students are ready to enter into a new unit, thinking about your role in helping students to get started in their personal work plan will pay off in setting the stage for introducing new concepts, knowledge, and competencies to them. When students know they have autonomy in their own learning and you take the time to coach them to learn how to take charge of completing their own quality work, you honor the agreement with your principal to support your own autonomy to take risks to change the way students work in your classroom.

For example, if you were to walk into either of our learning spaces where we teach, on most days you might not even notice that a teacher is in the room. When Michael first began to shift power to students, he found himself most often working on the level of the students, rather than standing and teaching at the dominant teaching wall.

For example, if you were to visit Michael teaching today, you will most often find him sitting with a student or a small group and either sharing feedback on their work or answering their questions while another group

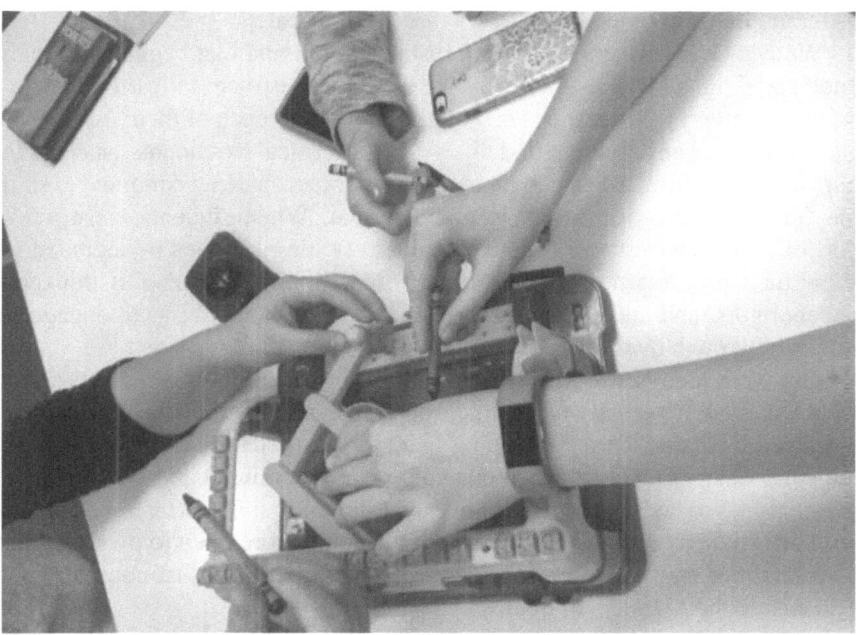

practices competencies of oral communication for a project they will present. You will observe him occasionally moving his attention to the group practicing for their presentation so he will be ready to move there next to hear their dialogue. Other students in his class may be reading or finding research sources for an upcoming project such as demonstrating the scientific concept of friction.

Both of us have shared publicly in conference presentations that shifting power to students doesn't mean that you as teacher stop structuring the learning space or the student work. In fact, when students are working at their own pace and on interest-driven content projects, the class organization may be more subtle to observe than when students sit in rows. However, the progressive approach to learning that we have adopted demands far more complex management strategies to support students to pace differently, work simultaneously on different activities, and create different project outcomes than to simply have them come in and sit in rows.

One strategy that can be helpful throughout the year is to have each student in the class and a parent sign a contract that a student will work at a different pace and that the students, at different times, may demonstrate their knowledge and competencies in a way that they choose. Establishing trust, respect, and knowledge of teacher/student expectations at the beginning of the year is essential to having students contract work they will accomplish at different points in time as they move through the year.

We want our learners to develop responsibility, and that begins with their understanding, as well as their parents; we expect learners to learn differently, but we always expect the best work possible from each of them.

We also see engagement in daily writing as critical to students' success in our classes. Writing is basic to almost every project students complete even if the final product is oral or in a video format. When students construct a portfolio of their best work, it's critical that writing samples be included to show their progress not just in terms of their writing, but also as thinkers, collaborators, and makers. This helps students and their parents to engage in assessing growth over time.

Our work today as educators represents a shift in our own mind-sets about what a class is supposed to look like, sound like, and be like when the culture is shaped by active learners learning in a more experiential approach than in our early days as teachers when our voices were dominant and student work was highly directed. As a result of our own mind-set shifts, which we discuss with our students, we notice that they too become more open to owning their own learning and making a more concerted effort to not just complete but also ensure their work is of quality.

THE LEARNING SPACE AND BEHAVIOR

We believe that students can help you designate workspaces set up explicitly to allow them to design, create, and make what they need for projects they complete throughout the year. Students may move to creation spaces as they need to work as long as they are not involved with a teacher in an activity or when a fellow student is presenting to the class.

For students to learn to exercise autonomy, they must begin to make choices among available learning options. This also means providing students with experiences in which they select for their own comfort while learning. Learning, especially new or challenging curricular content, is hard work and can be uncomfortable.

When we refer to comfort, we aren't just talking about physical, but also cognitive and social-emotional comfort. In learning, humans need to move. They need spaces for heads-down, individual learning at times, as well as well-constructed spaces for collaborative work. They need to work with people they trust and who trust them.

To optimize opportunities for individual success, the classroom must be set up to maximize flexibility not just in environmental design but also within the responsive learning culture. The role of the teacher in shaping learning spaces and classroom culture is pivotal to autonomy. This plays out in the daily interaction between teacher and learners as they learn to accommodate each other's needs, personalities, habits, and behaviors.

For example, there is occasionally a little "horseplay" or even loud chatting among students, neither of which is unusual among middle schoolers. To address this, you can first make eye contact as a prompt to check behaviors. If learners interrupt the flow of a lesson to such a degree that it keeps others from learning or you from teaching, you can use a second visual prompt no matter where you are located. This second eye contact with a student sends a message consistent with an already agreed upon protocol that the student will move his or her seat to wherever that student "will conduct their best work" (Erwin 2004).

This approach is consistent with William Glasser's choice theory that sets up opportunities for students to consider the choices they have to get basic needs satisfied: fun, freedom, and a sense of belonging are some examples. Learning to use choice theory as a social-emotional learning frame sets the stage for a culture in which misbehavior is addressed within the classroom community to maximize learning. Rather than looking to external rewards or consequences, in this model you spend time mentoring and coaching replacement behaviors rather than monitoring negative checkmarks, time-outs, and referrals to the office to consequence behaviors.

It's also a time when you can sit down and discuss the work. If a student says, "I hate math and this work is boring," what else do you need to know? Perhaps the student lacks skills or background knowledge to do the work. Maybe the student is being distracted by others. Or, maybe he or she can already do the work you've assigned.

By beginning with examining how you as the teacher can make changes, you may address the root cause of off-task or inappropriate behaviors rather than jumping in to address a behavioral cause. When a student and you realize that your effort to change the situation can result in a different outcome rather than a consequence, your mind-set about what you can accomplish grows in a positive direction.

In the application of choice theory, students learn that they are responsible for their own behavior individually and within the class community. This does not happen without spending time with learners to develop class norms and protocols for addressing what happens when a learner steps outside the norms.

Taking students through a process to learn choice theory takes about two weeks, in the beginning of the year, using role-play scenarios to implement how the teacher and students will work together to create a peaceful community. Students need to know the boundaries for classroom interactions, use of resources, and accomplishment of learning work. They need to be held responsible for their actions. However, we have learned from movement research that students especially need to be active.

Providing students with the freedom to move and to choose seating in which they will learn best is consistent with effective practices to support students to sustain attention, a life competency that is essential in many roles (Jensen 2005).

For example, we all have situations where we need to be quiet and attentive. Helping students, particularly those who need to be in motion, find strategies that work for them to handle times when they need to be quiet and focused provides them with accommodations to adapt to a variety of different classroom settings, work environments, and community activities.

If learners can't come up with their own strategies, as teachers we need to assist them. For example, when there is a need for quiet in the classroom or to sit and listen to a speaker, a student can use a sand ball to squeeze at his or her seat. This can help the student mindfully and quietly attend without calling attention to the action. As students learn to use accommodating strategies to stay connected with the learning and work within the classroom norms, they also are learning that their efforts pay off in the choices they make. This reinforces development of a growth mind-set that applies not just to cognitive learning but also social-emotional development ("The Growth Mindset—What Is Growth Mindset?" n.d.).

RESEARCH AND CHOICE

Are your students allowed to research a topic of interest to them as it arises? Do they need to ask you to use Google to find the answer to a question they may have? As we have explored student autonomy, we've come to believe that helping them to learn to do research is a key lifelong learning competency.

When students know *they* are responsible for *their* own learning and that *their* interests are as important to us as *their* learning the curriculum is to us, we begin to see learning sparks fly in the room. Using our facilitative roles to connect their interests to the prescribed curriculum, we begin to see capabilities and strengths emerge in our classrooms that we otherwise might not have seen.

We believe that our strategic focus to using students' interests to support them to develop research competencies leads to students who learn to think deeply within a choice-based learning model. However, this does not occur without a structural scheme for organizing instruction that leads to engaged learners.

For example, we have used this structural approach to a daily learning design:

- Create a daily agenda on the board that includes the time you've reasonably allocated to certain activities throughout class. Before students begin to work, ask them to look over the daily agenda and decide where each would like to begin.
- If some students choose reading, let them jump into the reading lesson. Others may need to access tech devices to do research for a project with a partner. However, if other students choose writing, you might provide "maker" time up front so they can create an artifact to incorporate into their writing. Students often need time to create, share, talk, and collaborate with each other prior to beginning to write. Maker time serves to warm students up for the activity they have chosen.
- Set a timer to monitor the activity so students don't exceed their allocated making time (be sure to include enough time for cleanup). You also can assign monitoring of the timer to a student with a cell phone. When some students may be in writing block, others may be researching information for projects, and you are working with a reading group to discuss an excerpt from the novel *Crossover*, which they are reading.
- Provide individual writing choices that students can access through the daily agenda, which may be on the interactive board or in a Google Doc. Would a student like to write a short story using irony (if that is the concept being learned), a chapter in his or her own book, or a book coauthored with others? If students don't know how to get started, you can encourage them to construct a poem, rap lyrics, or a script for a short video to show they know how to apply irony.

Cheryl also has used making to learn as an entry into writing with her students. This strategy is one that is applicable in elementary school, and it can be utilized in middle and in high school as well.

Fingers. If you observed students in Cheryl's class, you would see fingers flying across computer keys after students have opened their minds while "making." When a couple of students were asked in her class why they write better after "making," one student said, "I get out all the other thoughts in my head during 'making time' and my mind becomes more open to writing." Another student commented, "I make pictures using a paint program, sort of like in a graphic novel, and then when I've got my ideas, I'm ready to start writing dialogue using the pictures I just made."

Students need to learn the competencies of lifelong learning. They also need to learn to focus, prioritize, and problem solve to complete tasks. They need to think about the decisions they make and why.

With teachers modeling a growth mind-set, students can learn to consider choices including their commitment to making an effort to persevere to produce quality work. Students make that decision every day in schools. We believe it is better for students to make small mistakes in schoolwork and learn from those as a scaffold to making good and appropriate choices later on in adulthood.

CHOICE AND COMFORT

We consider our classrooms to be safe zones where no one laughs at or makes fun of anyone. Our classes aren't perfect either, but our focus is on learning and how students learn best with the support of their class community. It's important to model this behavior as well. Cheryl remembers sharing with her class that her leg fell asleep while a student was presenting, but that she knew to wait until the student finished to move to the side of the room and stand for a while. The students got that! They catch on to more than one can even imagine.

Students of all ages, even adults, value experiences where they can create resources that allow them to show their learning. When you first jump into setting up maker opportunities, you have to assess if there is enough variety of resources on the "maker" cart to meet the interests of each student in the class. The teacher doesn't have to have a lot of materials, just a variety. Switch out the variety periodically. Everyone loves choice. Let the students make choices with something as simple as figuring out what they need to make. This will teach skills to help ready them to make more important choices later on in life.

We used to think that everything in our classrooms needed to be purchased ready made for students. As we have shifted our own mind-sets, we've discovered that students can create project work for the classroom as well as project-based learning—both hands-on tasks but with different ends in mind. We have encouraged students to take over as much of the classroom as possible, and this can even be a money saver since teachers spend a lot of money out of their pocket on wall decorations, bulletin boards, and content posters.

Over time, we've watched peers decide, as we have, to encourage students to make everything, including bulletin board displays, because decorated bordering costs quite a bit. In elementary school, they've made alphabets to hang on the wall, and secondary students can easily construct content posters, math procedure flowcharts, activity prompts, and so much more. With easily accessible devices, they have 2D- and 3D-printed display artifacts to accompany specific units from Civil War medical instruments to images of presidents.

How do we fund or find the materials that give our students opportunities to make what they need for projects? Another mind-set that we have shifted is the idea that teachers have little control over obtaining resources they need beyond the basics. We have to acknowledge that we work in a district that

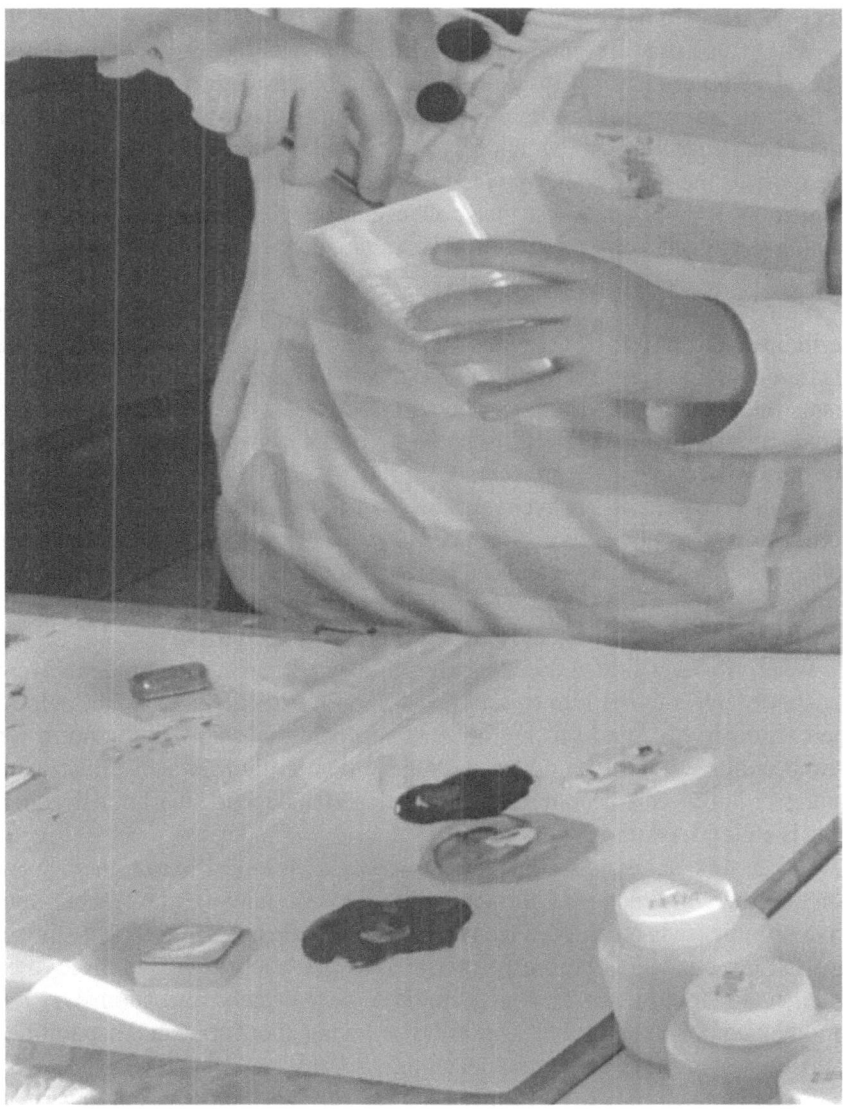

encourages edu-entrepreneurship, but we find teachers in our Twitter feed all over the country who are figuring out how to resource their classrooms.

For example, you can make a resource donation list in the beginning of the school year to share with parents or even neighbors, write a quarterly newsletter listing needed resources to share with parents, or set up a Donors-

Choose site (many teachers in economically disadvantaged schools use this since neither parents nor the school has resources).

We've also used a wish tree hung with stars that students have made and labeled with needed class resources. This can be set up during the beginning of the year when parents come in for open house, Back-to-School Night, or student-led conferences. Parents may take a star with an item listed on it and donate it to the classroom. We also have found amazing resources at local storefronts for organizations that collect and resell donations: cloth, trim, electrical gadgets, old toys even. These can be deconstructed and reconstructed by students into resources they need for projects.

You will find that items needed for the class "maker" cart disappear periodically from use by students. Replenishing the cart routinely keeps the creative work of the class running smoothly. Turning the cart over to student teams on a rotating schedule can be an effective way to keep the cart organized. Students can write letters home or to local school supply stores requesting what they need to restock.

You also can have a scavenger hunt list for students to find items at their homes or homes of relatives (with permission, of course). Students love the competition to find unique and interesting materials that they can donate for project use. The "prize" for their effort is actually having the materials with which to continue learning and hearing appreciation from peers.

When Michael first started teaching in elementary school, students were constantly interrupting him to ask questions, for directions, or to get help in their work. In his mind-set, he first just accepted that this was the norm for young children—until he added a strategy that shifted his sense that even young children can become self-directed and independent of the teacher. This is called "Ask three before me."

Using this strategy when students have a question about their work whether there are materials for something they are making, the teacher may have prompt cards on worktables labeled "Ask three before me!" The student can ask three students before he or she asks the teacher. We've discovered whether it's adolescents or young children, they usually find an answer before they come to the teacher. Our mind-set today about students' capabilities is different than when we started teaching.

Students need to independently practice solving problems on their own. Locating needed materials is one example. As a result of using this strategy, the teacher can continue important teaching work rather than being interrupted thirty times to respond to whether there are any more glue sticks left.

We've discussed the importance of students having choices of seating and work areas in their classrooms. How the class makes decisions under your guidance that results in choices is important to consider. In this example, students in upper elementary to high school can accomplish the task of arranging the space. With the intention of a space that's flexible enough to be rearranged periodically if not daily, at the beginning of the year you can move furniture into the center of the room.

During first block, ask students to stand while you explain to the class that they will have the chance to work together safely and cooperatively to arrange the room so it works best for each student in the class. You might need to set parameters including sharing a diagram that shows how they might approach setting up tables for small-group work, sustain access to natural light if you have a window, or create spaces for individual, quiet work.

You will need to discuss safety of moving couches, heavy chairs, et cetera. Some students will want to start moving furniture immediately while others may begin with a diagram. You will need to devote the full block of class and likely need to call time-out for the class to discuss where they are in the project and what still needs to be done. However, the task will need to be completed and the students seated prior to leaving.

Only the first block class can tweak the design for a couple days. The arrangement then is left that way, unless there is a safety issue. After three weeks, ask another class to arrange the room for how it works best for each of them. Students will continue to improve the redesign throughout the year, arranging the space to accommodate their needs.

It's always interesting to see the students realize how difficult it is to just move the couple pieces of furniture. It's a great opportunity to practice metacognitive strategies as the class moves into the school year. Did all students participate in problem solving? Were they cooperative? Did they pull together to make it happen? This is what adults do at work. Why not give students the opportunity to make the room their own and take responsibility for their own learning?

RESEARCH AND THE TWENTY-FIRST-CENTURY STUDENT

As the arrangement of the room has been altered, does the teacher alter his or her thinking by researching new and innovative best practices for teaching? What works best for the developmentally appropriate learning for the age of students you teach? Some research is what we call action research, and that occurs using data available to you in your own classroom as exemplified by qualitative observations, student portfolio, and performance tasks, and more decontextualized assessment data.

Finding researchers who are informing contemporary learning is a critical component of what teachers committed to making a difference do all the time. When you become knowledgeable of John Hattie's research (Killian 2017) on effect size of specific best practice strategies or Daniel Willingham's (Willingham 2009) focus on strategies that engage learners, or you "hang out" in Twitter to gather evidence-based resources from peers, your research on how to have the greatest impact on student learning is critical to students' success.

You also can do action research with your students to inform your thinking. What are the current applications students utilize on their iPhones? On their laptops? This research definitely can be used to your advantage because learning from your students makes your own commitment to learning something new more personal to them. Learning will become transactional with students as you transform a traditional classroom to one steeped in innovation and creativity. Such a learning design shift supports students to learn how to learn and help you do so as well.

To help accomplish this mind-set shift, your study of teaching techniques, tools, room arrangement, and classroom climate should delve deeply into contemporary research. Focus on more than strategies tied to improving academic progress. For example, the body of research on social-emotional learning (SEL) informs an area of significant need for students today. It's evident from contemporary research that students, particularly at-risk learners, achieve at higher academic levels and acquire SEL competencies when evidence-based SEL practices are used in their classrooms. Of SEL research sources, one of the best is the Collaborative for Academic, Social, and Emotional Learning (CASEL) ("SEL Impact," n.d.).

The use of technology in schools raises questions from our peer teachers and us about what constitutes appropriate and responsible use. However, the use of mobile devices and other technologies is here to stay, and most educators understand the importance of students' access to both current devices and applications that positively impact their learning.

We know there are many opinions about technology use by students, especially our younger elementary students. That's why we see Common Sense Media as one of the better sources of research information regarding digital citizenship and literacy as well as instructional strategies relevant to learning tech integration ("Common Sense Research," n.d.).

Today's students often know more than we do about technology applications. We should use that to our advantage toward their learning. For example, students might write a story in "Scratch," a programming language that went through research and development at MIT for use with young children. Students can also use "Kudo" and "Minecraft" to write stories, create historical virtual worlds, and construct social interpretations of settings from novels.

As students utilize a variety of lifelong learning competencies, you will find your relationships with students will deepen. For students to transfer learning into long-term memory, they need to practice and use what they learn in a variety of contexts, not just one. This happens when teachers plan for learning beyond the simple recall of facts, understanding connections to and implications for what they learn. When this happens, learning becomes fun, relevant, and meaningful.

You might ask what you would see in a classroom in which students are focused on learning outcomes that go beyond simply prepping for some version of state assessments. Our learners, whether kindergartners or seniors in high school, begin to practice and use lifelong learning competencies at an early age and continue working on those all the way to graduation. These competencies inform the work of classrooms and schools.

Students should apply and adapt a variety of appropriate strategies to solve new and increasingly complex problems. Furthermore, their use of habits of mind and strategies to plan, monitor, and evaluate their own work will also help them see their classrooms as spaces of risk, as opportunities in which student autonomy takes precedent over teacher direction, and as centers of research and development of best practices for learning.

Lifelong learning competencies such as conducting research, thinking critically, using precise language, and seeing learning through metacognition are important for each student to develop. When students in your classroom environment look like, sound like, and act like lifelong learners, your goal to engage their hearts and minds as learners together is made real. This is innovative thinking for the working world as well as fun for students while they learn.

WORKS CITED

"Common Sense Research." n.d. Common Sense Media. Accessed July 8, 2018. https://www.commonsensemedia.org/research.

Erwin, Jonathan. 2004. "Laying the Foundation for a Classroom of Choice." In *The Classroom of Choice*. Alexandria, VA: ASCD. http://www.ascd.org/publications/books/104020/chapters/Laying-the-Foundation-for-a-Classroom-of-Choice.aspx.

"The Growth Mindset—What Is Growth Mindset?" n.d. Mindset Works. Accessed July 3, 2018. https://www.mindsetworks.com/Science/.

"Improve Group Responding: Numbered Heads Together." n.d. Intervention Central. Accessed July 8, 2018. https://www.interventioncentral.org/cooperative_learning_numbered_heads_together.

Jensen, Eric. 2005. "Movement and Learning." In *Teaching with the Brain in Mind*. Alexandria, VA: ASCD. http://www.ascd.org/publications/books/104013/chapters/movement-and-learning.aspx.

Killian, Shaun. 2017. "Hattie's 2017 Updated List of Factors Influencing Student Achievement." Australian Society for Evidence Based Teaching. September 24, 2017. http://www.evidencebasedteaching.org.au/hatties-2017-updated-list/.

Marzano, Robert. 2010. "Representing Knowledge Nonlinguistically." *Educational Leadership* 67, no. 8 (May): 84–86. http://www.ascd.org/publications/educational-leadership/may10/vol67/num08/Representing-Knowledge-Nonlinguistically.aspx.

"SEL Impact." n.d. CASEL. Accessed July 8, 2018. https://casel.org/impact/.

Tallman, Melissa. 2014. "Expert Groups: A Cooperative Learning Strategy (Post 1 of 5)." *Teacher Thrive* (blog). July 28, 2014. https://teacherthrive.com/2014/07/expert-groups-cooperative-learning.html.

"Ten Metacognitive Teaching Strategies." n.d. Centre for Innovation and Excellence in Learning. Accessed July 8, 2018. https://ciel.viu.ca/teaching-learning-pedagogy/designing-your-course/how-learning-works/ten-metacognitive-teaching-strategies.

Willingham, Daniel. 2009. *Why Don't Students Like School?* San Francisco: Jossey-Bass.

Chapter Six

Creating a Vision

We too often consult our own convenience, rather than the comfort, welfare, or accommodation of our children.—William Alcott, 1832

QUESTIONS TO PONDER IN THIS CHAPTER

- *How does a school, or a school system, move from a system of compliance to a system of risk taking?*
- *Why is a systemic approach essential?*
- *What allows an administrator to create a revolutionary environment?*
- *What inspires revolution?*

CREATING A VISION: RISK MUST BE WHAT WE DO

Walking into one of our learning spaces, whether it is Michael's K–5 multi-age room, Cheryl's seventh-grade language arts room, or Ira's university halls (or even his office spaces), it is easy to see chaos. Unlike traditional spaces, students move freely; sit in a variety of seats, in all kinds of furniture; use school computers and/or personal phones; or write on paper. They choose what tasks to work on.

The essence of this learning space form is creating those spaces for risk. Does this spot work for this task? Is this the best way to get from where I am to where I want to be? Will saying this in public expose me to ridicule?

But this is essential: when risk is less than systemic, the result is "that crazy teacher down the hall," or "you are *so* lucky that your kid got *that* teacher," and this is the standard state of failure in our schools. Yet for over a century and a half the education system in both the United States and the nations of the former British Empire have been moving steadily toward the systemization of risk aversion; shifting from a theme of colonization as assimilation of cultural differences into the dominant culture to one of mass standardization (Zhao 2015).

This systemization mostly occurred during the early twentieth-century shift from an agrarian to an industrial economy when communities selected to close one-room schoolhouses and move to a factory school model that educated a few for postsecondary education and many for blue-collar work in urban factories and small mill towns across the United States.

Students moved from the one-room schoolhouse model of multiage collaborative learning based on a daily school schedule set by the needs of families for their children to help with farmwork to one driven by a bell schedule, age-based grade levels, desks in rows, and one teacher teaching many students in classrooms that followed the same Committee of Ten recipe for curriculum across the nation (Eliot, Hill, and Winship 1894).

Compliance became the norm in schools, not the exception, because students needed to learn to obey the boss on the factory floor, accomplish the repetitive work of assembly lines, be on time for work, and take breaks as directed. The goal was to create a workforce that learned the same basics to prepare them for blue-collar work.

For generation after generation, administrators have risen from the ranks of compliant teachers, as teachers have risen from the ranks of compliant students. Success, in our educational systems, is graded on compliance: you did your homework, you crammed for the test, you turned in your grades on time, your classroom wasn't too noisy, and parents didn't complain.

Risk is thus a truly revolutionary idea—a dangerous idea, a threatening idea—within the doors of the schoolhouse. Changing education, however, requires school boards to allow superintendents to take risks, superintendents to allow principals to take risks, principals to allow teachers to take risks, IT directors to allow teachers and students to take risks, and, of course, teachers to allow students to take risks. To take true root, to impact every child, requires risk-taking behavior to cascade down from the top while being celebrated daily from the bottom up.

This vision of risk begins with a very simple statement: "We trust children and childhood." That is, we trust curiosity, exploration, trial and error, play, mistakes, big mistakes, dawdling, doodling, dirt, mud, scrapes, falls, climbs, hiding, noise, caves, inventions, making yourself comfortable, and doing what no one expected you to do.

ALL OF THAT

This represents a comprehensive vision built on a long series of small "unlearnings" on the part of teachers and administrators—small unlearnings, but complicated unlearnings of culture, structure, and identity that were driven into the essence of what it meant to be an educator over generations. To unlearn means that educators have to deeply study how we arrived at the current state of practice in our schools and to take the risk to change those practices in a purposeful way with an end in mind.

Rote memorization, for example, was the dominant outcome of learning defined by the Committee of Ten to standardize the course of study implemented in the early 1900s and taken to the next level with standardized assessments that measured student acquisition of defined standards promulgated by states in response to federal mandates in 2001.

To "unlearn" the memorization model means taking risks to move away from a vision of learning driven by mass standardization to one driven by mass customization as Yong Zhao has described it. This means developing curriculum, assessment, and instruction that is reflective of local communities and the differentiated needs and interests of learners who will work in a global economy, live in diverse communities, and make homes, all filled with new, smart technologies.

The old outcomes associated with factory floor compliance are the antithesis of the new outcomes learners need to take with them into life after high school: critical thinking, creativity, a continuum of communication competencies, and the capability to work collaboratively in diverse teams.

One "unlearning" start to what we accept as a vision for schooling can be found in literature, as exemplified in the book and films *Lord of the Flies*. This staple of middle school fiction is not about the dangers of children—especially boys—returning to a hazardous natural state. Rather, it is a book by an English government schoolteacher who writes a caustic indictment of the British public school (elite private school) system and the horrors imparted by those schools on the boys of the ruling class, the "boys" who had just led Britain into and through a world war.

Lord of the Flies describes the vicious structure of English society. The choir has been taught that they are elite and above doubt. All the boys are taught that physical weakness—Piggy—or even empathy for physical weakness—Ralph—is unacceptable. Eugenics—the beliefs in the inherent uselessness to society of many, so popular in the UK, US, Germany, and Japan in the first third of the twentieth century—is as key a part of the story, as is the rejection of democracy by a society under stress. It is easy to see Ralph, Piggy, and their group representing the unschooled, or unsuccessfully schooled, and the choir representing the star students—the ruling class (Conrad 2009).

Yet, in America, this book is always taught in mirror image, as a way of justifying brutal schooling. Without the rule of adults, teachers all across the nation tell seventh and eighth graders, children descend into dangerous anarchy. Thus, seats in rows and enforced silence, closed classrooms and large amounts of homework, fully scheduled days and long lists of rules all become a method of adult protection of children, and all developed in the early twentieth century in response to the need for a tiered school system that would feed workers to the factories so in need of compliant workers.

First, our myths must go. *Lord of the Flies* and a hundred other book and film variations of the "dangerous" child in need of teachers who have been advised "Don't smile for the first half of the school year" must be reanalyzed as part of the unlearning process. Then, our belief in "the dangerous world" of childhood must go as well. In reality, American children have never been safer. Most deadly childhood diseases have vanished. Automobiles are shockingly safe transports.

Homes are babyproofed and childproofed. In the place of these real dangers, *we* parents and educators have invented a thousand crises—from dangerous playgrounds to cancer-causing soccer fields, from tipping chairs to cell phone dangers, from being outside to being even momentarily out of sight. Wrapped in bubble wrap, controlled by a list of rules, children are forced to remain fully dependent on their adults. We lament our teens aren't independently ready to enter the world of college, work, or community but, in reality, they are ready—to remain as dependent upon adults as we have taught them to be.

Finally, the myth of "school as preparation for school" must vanish. In the US, almost every student is told that the reason for school being controlling, boring, unfair, and painful is that they are being prepared for the next level of education. "Although homework may not immediately affect the achievement of children in grades K through five, many teachers and parents agree that homework helps to develop children's initiative and responsibility—attributes that play a vital role in their long-term academic development—and fulfills the expectations of students, parents, and the public. Homework helps younger children develop the strong study skills necessary for high academic achievement later," writes Linda Milbourne and David Haury in the *Eric Review*, reinforcing the notion that purpose of school is school—a very common meme (Milbourne and Haury 1999).

With all these myths, we hold children captive for thirteen years in a system that not only has no relation to their real lives but wipes their real lives out by seizing most waking hours from the natural life of a child or teen. There is little time for curiosity or exploration, for the kind of learning play that truly builds the brain. With these myths we ignore children's needs while insisting that they pay attention to our needs. However, school staff can change this paradigm—but it requires creation of a different vision for teaching and learning, one grounded in a progressive viewpoint that the structures of schools be child determined, not educator driven ("Mission/Vision," n.d.).

We seem to have forgotten in the United States that young children learn best through structured *and* unstructured play. Adolescents need significant time with adult coaches and mentors as well as experiential opportunities to develop social-emotional skills essential in communities, and teens need the chance to work side by side with adults as apprentices to acquire the transitional competencies essential to soon being on their own.

We have over many decades created a vision for educating young people that may have helped the nation transition from an agrarian to an industrial workforce, but it is not the vision we need for this century's learners.

A vision shouldn't be negative, though, and so as we clear out the destructive myths we must build our library of stories of real childhood. Those stories surround us and fill our memories. What did it feel like to first climb a tree? Ride a bike? Swim across a pool? Hit a baseball? Hear an amazing story? Watched a movie that changed your life? Told a story that your listeners loved?

Think about the way toddlers learn—how they grasp everything, taste everything, and smell everything. Think about how they engage all senses to learn everything about anything. How they are natural investigators and natural explorers.

Think of the joy you observe when you see children master something new that they've accomplished without adult help, of the power of a group of kids solving some problem together. How about your own wonder when you watch a child do something you didn't think he or she could do?

The vision you need to create schools and classrooms with space for risk will be built on those stories rather than ones of compliance, standardization,

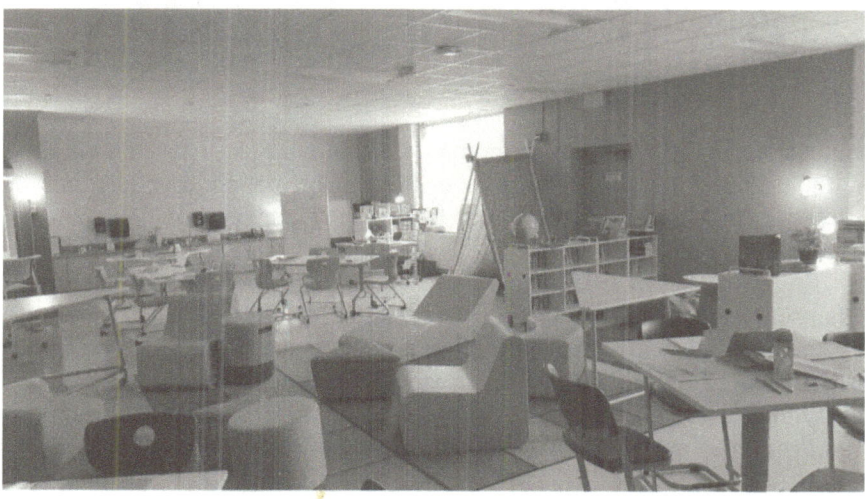

and accountability that have been the dominant narrative of vision building in the twentieth century. Now imagine your images of children learning for success in life in their century, not that of their parents and grandparents. That will not happen by chance.

To get started on articulating a vision for contemporary learning means educators have to step outside the boxes called schools and leave behind the structural efficiencies and curricula that have prescribed what it means to become educated for the last 120 years. This certainly doesn't mean that everything educators have done for decades must be rejected. It does mean that everything must be questioned, observed, and researched.

In the district and schools where we work, this means that educators must begin with their own need to become educated about the world outside our schools; the range of educational perspectives of stakeholders from across the community; the knowledge basis about changes occurring in homes, society, and work as we move into the fourth industrial revolution also known as the smart machine age; and, of course, the breadth and depth of brain science research about how children learn.

The steps we believe are critical to developing a desired-state vision based on current-state knowledge are represented in what is known as the plan-do-study-act (PDSA) continuous improvement cycle for determining needed organizational changes and a rationale for why those are necessary. However, this visioning work begins with a design thinking process that embeds PDSA tools so that the design process can move vision from words on a website or school wall to vibrant implementation in every classroom of a school.

A school without shared vision is one in which staff will implement what they know from their own schooling. They will not establish a common direction for the learning work students do, but rather will act with no direction, confusing parents and students alike as to what is important to learn and why. Even if a school has a long-standing vision, it is important to revisit it periodically against current state information and data to determine if progress on student learning outcomes aligns with the vision and, quite frankly, if the vision and outcomes are still relevant.

To do the work of creating vision means far more in-depth study than we can share in this chapter, but here are some process steps to help frame the work that lies ahead to build shared vision in your district or school (Gabriel and Farme 2009):

1. The need to create a vision and/or review a current vision must be triggered through the established communication structures and processes in place in your school. This means using those to reach out to stakeholders in a variety of ways to find out their perspectives on what they believe, value, and think as they consider the purpose of education for today's children. When this process gets triggered through surveys, focus groups, established advisory groups, and informal conversations, you can bet that people will have some angst about why anything needs to change. It's important that leaders of this process listen reflectively to stakeholders and have a clear rationale that can be shared as to why visioning or re-visioning is needed in the school.

2. It's important to establish a diverse steering team who will lead and offer perspective throughout the visioning process. This team must determine what processes will be used, and a first essential task is researching design thinking models to select one that can be used to facilitate the hard work, the committed and time-intensive work, that it takes to arrive at a shared vision

that will then trigger the actions necessary to implementing any changes that emerge as necessary from the visioning process.

We have worked with the IDEO human-centered/educational design thinking toolkit ("Design Thinking for Educators," n.d.) as well as the Stanford d.school equity model for reimagining schools ("Equity-Centered Design Framework," n.d.). What is most important about the design thinking process is that it must reflect a responsiveness to the needs and desires of those who are on the user end of the vision—the learners.

3. Once you have a steering team established, trained in the process, and ready to begin working through the design thinking model with stakeholders, it's important to make their work public, so establishing a website where the team can archive curated articles, online research, video resources, and minutes from meetings will help make the visioning process transparent to your community.

It's important that all voices of the community be represented in the visioning process and that each iteration of gathering perspectives that curated background knowledge of why the process was triggered be shared—research on changing demographics, contemporary workforce information, brain research relevant to how children learn, and student data regarding learning, attendance, discipline, engagement, school climate, and postsecondary status can reinforce the successes of a school as well as create dissonance regarding the current state. This is an opportunity to begin the "unlearning" that can lead from what schools are to what schools could be as profiled in Ted Dintersmith's book about his journeys to search for America's innovative schools (Dintersmith 2018).

4. As the steering team moves through the processes they have identified to arrive at a short vision that is commonly shared and descriptive of the purposeful learning outcomes held dear in general by stakeholders, they also need to be focused on the plan-do-study-act model as a frame for continuous improvement essential to making the vision a reality in every classroom. This model represents a four-stage cycle that must be embedded in all the work that follows the establishment of vision:

- Plan: What change initiatives are necessary for implementing the vision, and why are they critical priorities? These initiatives likely will involve determining a sequence of needs and a strategic plan including but not limited to professional learning, curriculum, assessment, technology uses, space redesign, student-teacher relationships, and communication.
- Do: How will staff strategically implement initiative priorities by aligning the plans and actions to implement the plan as a system of deep change, not a onetime event of superficial change? The team will need to communicate clearly to all those touched by the plan what changes will occur and why those changes will occur in support of the vision. For example, if the

vision includes a focus on acquiring competencies relevant to lifelong learning for success in work and community, then using a project-based learning (PBL) model to develop collaboration and critical thinking competencies may make sense. However, to accomplish this, staff will need to adapt their pedagogies to integrate PBL into their planning, pacing, and mapping of the year. This should be grounded in ongoing professional development (PD) that will demand time and resources to raise the level of expertise among teachers.

- Study: In what ways will data be collected to inform progress toward meeting the learning goals that align with the vision? We've seen initiatives come and go occasionally that may or may not be tied to the school's vision. Sometimes teachers have no sense of why an initiative has been put into place even if the administrators do. It's not uncommon in America's schools for staff to go through the school year, some choosing to implement and some ignoring an initiative. Everyone has attended required "sit and get" PD to learn how to implement the initiative only to never be involved in any assessment of its outcomes whether formative or summative. In the study phase, data and information are collected that align the initiative with the vision and goals that everyone has already agreed to own. Implementers get ongoing opportunities to provide and receive feedback. Formative data are collected and shared with stakeholders and implementers. Summative data are gathered systematically and used to inform next steps for initiative implementation. The work becomes part of a flow of change to make the vision real.
- Act: Now that we have formative and summative data, both qualitative and quantitative, to inform next steps in the PDSA cycle, how do we make further improvements to change structures and practices? For example, if staff have implemented school-wide PBL with students (and this can be at any level) and they discover that some teachers are providing students with a continuum of project choices but others tend to direct students toward one specific project, how do we use that data to make sense of this? With all variables held as constant as possible, you've found that student self-reports of their learning engagement are higher when they have choice in their project work than in classes that are more teacher directed. This is the time to create dissonance through data (remember that everyone said that if the vision was realized, learner engagement would be higher) as a mechanism to trigger change in practice. In this phase, staff doesn't just talk the talk of alignment of their work to change, but they actually make changes to better align with the vision, kicking everyone back to the first stage of the PDSA cycle.

Changing the vision is the easy part despite the time-intensive nature of engaging the full community of stakeholders. Challenging traditions of practice to make changes that align with a new vision is far more difficult. This does not happen in a day, a month, or even a year. It happens one educator at a time, each going through the unlearning process essential to his or her need for change. Imagine, however, a school community that embraces the changes necessary to making a shared vision real. Now, envision that it is your school.

WORKS CITED

Conrad, Peter. 2009. Review of *William Golding: The Man Who Wrote* Lord of the Flies, by John Carey. *Guardian*, August 29, 2009. http://www.theguardian.com/books/2009/aug/30/william-golding-john-carey-review.

"Design Thinking for Educators." n.d. IDEO. Accessed July 8, 2018. https://www.ideo.com/post/design-thinking-for-educators.

Dintersmith, Ted. 2018. *What School Could Be: Insights and Inspiration from Teachers across America*. Princeton, NJ: Princeton University Press.

Eliot, Charles W., Frank A. Hill, and A. E. Winship. 1894. "The Report of the Committee of Ten." *Journal of Educational Research* 40, no. 5 (979) (July): 91–93.

"Equity-Centered Design Framework." n.d. Stanford d.school. Accessed July 8, 2018. https://dschool.stanford.edu/resources/equity-centered-design-framework.

Gabriel, John G., and Paul C. Farme. 2009. *How to Help Your School Thrive without Breaking the Bank*. Arlington, VA: ASCD.

Milbourne, Linda A., and David L. Haury. 1999. "Why Is Homework Important?" ERIC Review 6 (2): 11–12. http://www.academia.edu/1770264/Why_is_Homework_Important.

"Mission/Vision." n.d. PEN—Progressive Education Network. Accessed July 8, 2018. https://progressiveeducationnetwork.org/mission/.

Zhao, Yong. 2015. "A World at Risk: An Imperative for a Paradigm Shift to Cultivate 21st Century Learners." Zhao Learning. April 6, 2015. http://zhaolearning.com/2015/04/06/a-world-at-risk-an-imperative-for-a-paradigm-shift-to-cultivate-21st-century-learners1/.

Chapter Seven

Sharing the Vision

The only thing worse than being blind is having sight but no vision.
—Helen Keller

QUESTIONS TO PONDER IN THIS CHAPTER

- *Why does there need to be a vision?*
- *Once a vision is created, what is the best way to share that vision with the school staff and community?*
- *Why is a shared vision important?*
- *How can a shared vision help promote a space for risk?*

THE VISION

How do you envision learning? What do you see when you imagine your ideal? What do you hope to watch your children do? What will your children know, what will they be able to do, when they leave you? If your vision replicates your school experience, you have fallen into a failure trap—you will continue a system in which, even by its own best measures, only one-third of children reach their potential ("NAEP Mathematics and Reading Highlights" 2017).

How do you build a vision that changes those results? How do you expand the universe of school "winners" to all learners preparing them for a future that looks nothing like the past?

As discussed in chapter 6, creating a vision is an imperative part of the process of using a design thinking model and the plan-do-study-act cycle (Strutchens and Iiams 2016).

Without a vision that establishes a sense of purpose for learning, school staff go in multiple directions and may even work at cross purposes. As addressed in chapter 6, a common vision brings staff, students, and community together. A great vision is thorough enough that the entire school community is clear on the expectations for the school, but brief enough and written in clear language so that anyone touched by the vision can articulate it in simple words.

A vision for contemporary learning must also operationally define how the school community will move toward creating a space for risk. The vision should articulate through its words that a space for risk is important and worth the time and effort of staff and learners. People process a vision statement differently based on their experience, their openness to the vision, and their own processing speed. For some, periodic, focused conversation in a staff meeting may be enough while others may need more detailed explanation through in-depth development. Either way, creation of the vision is well worth the time and commitment that it takes to develop it.

Vision statements can take many forms and may be more or less abbreviated based on the consensus of those with input into it. Bob Pearlman, one of the creators of the New Tech Network, has curated and shared vision statements online from several school districts that he believes capture the essence of educating young people in this century ("21st Century School Districts Mission and Vision Statements," n.d.). He includes our district's verb-powered vision among those: "All learners believe in their power to embrace learning, to excel, and to own their future."

Once the vision is created, sharing the final product with staff, students, and community is critical. Communication must occur at all levels. The staff should actively promote and articulate the vision to students through day-to-day learning activities. They must model the vision every day through their planning and implementation of learning experiences for the students they serve. If staff members are unclear and unsupportive of the vision, that will spill over to the students and be evident in their classrooms.

If the vision speaks to the big idea—that students will actively learn through experiences that engage them in collaborative teams, and in working together they acquire essential knowledge, think critically and analytically, design, create and make as a team, and communicate the output of their learning work—then this can be seen in classes up and down halls and throughout the school.

Teachers will discuss in their professional learning community meetings how they are using strategies to elicit this work and the results from student assessments. As the principal plans faculty meetings with staff leaders, completes daily learning walks of classrooms, and digs in on formative and summative data, he or she can note examples and stories representative of the vision to share with others including parents, district office staff, and staff in the school.

In turn, students also must understand the relationship of their work to the school's vision. If teachers are the architects of the vision, then students are the ambassadors of the vision, and as they design, create, and share their work, it makes the vision real.

Their projects—writing, videos, websites, performances, expositions, and portfolios—become a living vision for parents and the community, not just through student project work but also through public-facing assessment data for the school. When students embrace the vision because it is embedded in their learner experiences, they become internally motivated to see it blossom through their work ("Learning Experience Design—The Most Valuable Lessons," n.d.). Concomitantly, if learners and staff do not believe in the vision, it will simply remain words on a wall or website.

The community also should find value in the school's new vision. Why? Even if community members do not have children in school, and many do not, they need young people to graduate with the competencies essential to being contributing members of the community and citizenry, good employees, and functional family members. For example, the elderly grandmother who needs skilled nursing care has a vested interest in having a certified nursing assistant and local high school graduate who delivers quality care. Citizens who are taxpayers want to know that the money that moves from their pockets to schools is paying off in students who are learning what they need to be successful in school and beyond.

Chapter 7
PREPARING TO SHARE THE VISION

How the vision is shared and articulated is as important as its creation in the first place. If the vision is shared in an ineffective way, it could potentially ruin any chance of creating a space for risk. First impressions are very important. The vision, created with input from stakeholders, will create a buzz when it is rolled out. People, especially staff, will be looking to see what will happen next. Even though initially this will be an exciting time, the buzz and excitement will lessen as the work begins to implement the vision.

When our district's vision was created with a focus on developing student agency and ownership for learning, the superintendent worked hard with staff to align professional development, curriculum, assessment, instruction, and resources with the vision. To educate the public and staff about the vision change, the vision statement was placed at the beginning of every PowerPoint slideshow. During development of the budget to support schools, this question was asked in every budget meeting: "How will this support our vision for learning?"

Over time, as more and more staff implemented learning experiences consistent with the vision, opportunities to tell the story through local media emerged and the division worked with schools to be sure we collected stories and used them as a chance to promote vision work.

When social media emerged as a more informal communication tool, teachers and administrators across our district, including us, began to share classroom images and videos (with parental permission) consistent with the vision in Twitter, Facebook blog posts, and more. Human resources staff aligned structures such as observation look-fors in the teacher performance appraisal plan. Central instructional staff worked with teacher teams to develop district curricula and a performance assessment model reflective of the vision.

Professional development was redefined around needs that teachers recommended that helped them incorporate best practices into their work to make the vision a reality. Even the capital improvements projects became expressions of the district vision such as the flexible, multiage school environment in which Michael completed his most recent teaching assignment. Even eight years after the district vision was created and rolled out, school and district staff still work collaboratively to implement teaching strategies and school structures that support attainment of the vision.

School administrators also must be prepared for school community members who are not supportive of the school vision. These individuals should be treated with respect. However, the principal must stay the course to implement strategies that support the vision while working to build the capacity of staff to move forward. Change is hard, and people will accept it at different times for different reasons.

There will also be some individuals who believe the new vision and direction of the school are not the right ones. It is close to impossible to convince or persuade everyone that the vision is the correct path to take. Remember that not everyone will buy in at the same time in the same manner.

The principal who commits the time to the hard work of engaging with those who are resistant to the vision may eventually help them start to consider at least trying out strategies representing change. The district vision for our schools uses strong verbs of action to describe—"embrace learning, excel, own their future"—its vision that learners will develop value for learning, excellence in their work, and a belief that they can attain their hopes and dreams for the future they want.

The beginning of the school year is a great time to start a new journey. It's logical to kick off the new school year with the new vision. But for that to happen effectively, the vision must be introduced the year before. In most cases, teachers have about one week to prepare lesson plans and set up their classrooms before the students' first day of school. That is not nearly enough time to truly engage staff in deconstructing their role in articulating the new vision.

Ideally, the administrator would use the prior year to prepare teacher leaders to introduce staff to the new vision. This builds momentum. Allowing them the time to make sense of how it will impact peers on their teams sets the stage for them to own the vision. They understand how important it is for staff to have opportunities to ask questions, build acceptance, and develop how they plan to together, and roll out the vision in the classroom. Teacher leaders also can partner with the principal to delineate why the changes are needed to align teachers' work with the vision and where the "potholes" may be that will impact implementation.

The principal must strategically place teacher leaders throughout teams so that the new vision is ready to be represented in learning work throughout the entire school. This means some staff may need to change their grade-level teams to address the leadership needs of the school community.

In addition to the work completed during the previous year, team leaders likely will need to spend a portion of their summer preparing for the upcoming year. Preparation is key. Every team leader should be ready to share and model the new vision to the staff, working collaboratively with peers to help their teammates begin to implement shifts in practice.

Each team leader should receive a financial stipend for the time they spend planning and leading the vision work. Their dedication to the new direction of the school will play a critical role in the success of the vision. Receiving some financial support for taking on a leadership role reinforces the importance of the role to them and others—not as a reward but to simply recognize the people who are willing to step up and teach the vision.

Once the vision is introduced to the entire staff, the administration will partner with the team leaders to help build a positive outlook. Beside the team leaders, the school administrator should have at least one teacher who can be viewed as an "expert" on the potential changes. This teacher might need to be brought in from another school, or they could already be teaching at the school. This particular teacher does not have to have a specific title or accolade, but their leadership will shine through their actions.

This teacher leader will be the school administrator's go-to on the front line of learning. When selecting this teacher, it is imperative that this teacher is fully on board with the direction of the school. Do not choose someone based solely on their past work. Be sure that this teacher fully understands the direction of the school and is invested in the new vision.

The bond formed between the teacher and the administrator over the vision of the school will be very important if it gets challenging. Since the teachers are working directly with the students and the vision, their perspective is vital. Administrators should keep an open mind during the process and be ready to answer questions about the vision.

SHARING THE VISION WITH THE STAFF

At the first faculty meeting of the year, the administrator should introduce the vision to the entire staff. The team leaders should be standing side by side with the administrator presenting the new vision. It is standard fare to have some sort of presentation created as a vehicle for sharing. Even though PowerPoint (PPT) slides seem to be the usual presentation tool at a typical faculty meeting, we believe using a PPT presentation will undermine the push for a space for risk. This is a time to tell stories and share images that inspire teachers to see themselves as capable of changing the narrative of schooling.

It also starts a discussion about strategies being advanced to support the new vision. They can converse about why those strategies are designed to lead students to ever-higher levels of performance—in the case of our district's vision, through project-based learning, maker work, interactive technologies, connectivity, universal design for learning, choice and comfort, and instructional tolerance.

When administration and teacher leaders plan the rollout of the vision, developing an unconventional method for sharing the vision will catch the attention of staff. One school leadership opened the year with a New Year's party focused on resolutions for a fresh approach to learning consistent with the vision. Another school showed video interviews with students sharing what they love about school: having fun; being active, engaged learners; pursuing their hopes and dreams for their own lives—and then the teacher

Sharing the Vision

leaders led teams through a protocol to discuss how what the students value aligned with the new vision.

The simple act of engaging staff with the vision shows them that the new vision is not just words. It is not just something new that will be discussed at the beginning of the year and forgotten halfway through the year. It will demonstrate from the start that the administration and team leaders are willing to take risks and to acknowledge that likely there will be challenges along the way.

Besides providing teachers with time to prepare their individual classrooms, the entire preservice week should be spent preparing staff for the new direction of the school. Over the summer, the principal should plan the preservice week agenda and professional development sessions tied to introducing new strategies. Using team leaders to facilitate the sessions so that teachers get their hands on the vision work allows staff to experience the new instructional practices that will be expected during the year.

The planning team must set up sessions that challenge traditional teaching practices and involve teachers in the adoption process. Using protocols (we tend to use protocols from High Tech High) that set the stage for diverse

members of faculty to converse and share with each other through collaborative conversations is basic to the professional development design for learning ("Protocols," n.d.).

We see several components of planning as critical to developing quality learning for adults working in schools:

- Define what the planning team would agree upon as the outcome for each "vision quest" session that will be offered given different levels of readiness among staff members.
- Set the stage immediately in each session to engage staff members through an activity in which they build a response to a key question. For example, if the goal of the vision quest session is to focus on interactive engagement of learners in a lesson, then teacher teams might use maker materials to build a model for what engagement means to them.
- After quick engagement of teacher teams, introduce them to the featured strategy by modeling three different approaches to engaging students. For example, the planning team might select a metacognitive strategy such as reflective journaling, collaborative problem solving through think-pair-share, and a peer partner cowriting strategy to create story dialogue.
- Teacher teams can work through these using a cooperative learning jigsaw in which they first learn one of the three strategies and then reconfigure to teach the strategy to peers.
- After the teams finish, they can debrief what they see as the challenges of using the strategies, how they plan to try out the strategies, who they plan to team with to observe a peer using the strategy, and in what ways they can assess impact on learners. By setting a goal for every staff member to use at least one of the three strategies on the first day back with students, the staff begins to develop a collective commitment to aligning practices with the new vision.

Basically, these well-designed, risk-taking professional development sessions will show the staff how to develop lessons that push students to take risks. These sessions will be pivotal in setting the stage for the year. Each teacher leader should push to design lessons that truly demonstrate a space for risk. Even if a lesson falls flat, it will be a good learning experience for all involved.

A SHARED VISION

Sharing the vision is not enough. There needs to be a transition from a vision being shared to having a shared vision. A shared vision signifies a community effort. It is not just a top-down initiative. It is an effort by all to make the changes that are necessary to realizing the vision by moving it from invention to strategic to operational work. Having the ability to envision the future for an institution is the sign of a good leader. Regardless, vision does not belong to any one person but to everyone. Developing and instituting a new vision is a joint venture of teachers and administrators.

If the vision is not spread throughout the school with all sharing the responsibility, it could fail. A shared vision implies that most involved are invested in the vision for the school. This commitment is needed so that the vision has a genuine opportunity to be successful. The buy-in from the staff will help foster the vision, which can directly lead to new instructional methodologies for the school.

The goal of the vision is to promote and push a pedagogical approach that meets needs of learners regardless of their current levels of skills and background knowledge. When developed and shared effectively, a space for risk can be created. It is not easy to take risks professionally, but it becomes easier for each staff member when the vision is shared and agreed upon. A shared vision creates more confidence, and that helps everyone involved to feel more comfortable with the decisions they make.

In turn, when teachers are more confident in their risk-taking decisions, that mind-set will trickle down to the students. Students will see the risks their teachers are making, and it will influence them to take learning risks as well. Furthermore, teachers will create lessons that challenge students to choose from opportunities that the teacher offers them and make decisions that help them learn at their individual level.

When students come to invest in the vision of the school, that often occurs as an outcome of classroom teachers who have relinquished much of their traditional control over the learning space. Once this happens, students and the teacher will begin to work more side by side instead of working on two different levels. The teacher will still be the authority in the classroom, but instructional decisions can and should be shared with the learners. These simple but challenging changes will help foster a space for risk.

WORKS CITED

"Learning Experience Design—The Most Valuable Lessons." n.d. The Interaction Design Foundation. Accessed July 8, 2018. https://www.interaction-design.org/literature/article/learning-experience-design-the-most-valuable-lessons.

"NAEP Mathematics and Reading Highlights." 2017. National Assessment of Educational Progress. 2017. https://www.nationsreportcard.gov/reading_math_2017_highlights/.

"Protocols." n.d. High Tech High Graduate School of Education. Accessed July 8, 2018. https://hthgse.edu/crei/protocols/.

Strutchens, Marilyn, and Michele Iiams. 2016. "A Deeper Dive into Plan-Do-Study-Act Cycles and Measures." Presented at the Mathematics Teacher Education Partnership conference, Washington, DC. http://www.aplu.org/projects-and-initiatives/stem-education/SMTI_Library/a-deeper-dive.pdf.

"21st Century School Districts Mission and Vision Statements." n.d. BobPearlman.org. Accessed July 8, 2018. http://www.bobpearlman.org/Learning21/Mission%20and%20Vision.htm.

Chapter Eight

Changing the Learning Space

Creativity is seeing what others see and thinking what no one else has ever thought.—Albert Einstein

QUESTIONS TO PONDER IN THIS CHAPTER

- *How might you facilitate "do-it-yourself" changes in space design from your perspective whether teacher, support specialist, or administrator?*
- *What spaces in your school are ready for a change in design, and how might readiness for that change be assessed?*
- *If you are going to change space in one way tomorrow, what will it be?*
- *What one changing space resource have you researched that you can share with peers or school leaders?*
- *Why change space in your school?*

LEARNER RESPONSIVENESS

School leaders often are challenged to use different skill sets when confronted with the need to shift the design of learning spaces in a school from the traditions of the twentieth century to new ways of meeting the learning needs of contemporary students. Young people today have been born into a digital world, one in which they have held devices in their hands since they were literally babies. All the children in our schools today were born in the twenty-first century. They have been entertained by technological toys and used even more sophisticated devices to engage in early learning.

They have grown up with smart technologies that allow them to stay connected 24/7 with friends and family members and to extend their social networks through chat rooms, social media connections, and virtual communication environments from YouTube to Instagram to Snapchat and through so many more apps that emerge almost daily.

In other words, children in our schools today, Generation Z or the phygitals (physical plus digital) as they have been labeled, expect school to be a space of social community where they can engage and learn together and apart. Older learning technologies—books, paintbrushes, hammers, and pencils—are still very useful in their education, but the range of tools available today extends the learning potential of Generation Z far beyond what has ever been available at any time in human history.

To advantage this potential, learning spaces must change to meet the needs of the contemporary learner differently than students in the last century.

Spaces must account for the range of experiences that will prepare children to be successful in life, not just to pass the tests that we have used to define success in school over recent decades. This means that school leaders and teachers must work together to ensure that as pedagogies, curriculum, and assessment shift in response to the changing paradigm of learning expectations, the spaces inside and outside of the school environments must shift as well.

Indeed, the overarching goal for space redesign and change must be to provide opportunities for children at any learning age to work alone, in small groups, and in larger gatherings on projects that represent personal interests, curricular-directed standards, and "whole-child" developmental needs. In our expectations for students, social-emotional, cognitive, and psychomotor development are all important and student interests and curriculum direction do

not need to be mutually exclusive, but optimally integrated as teachers notice learners and then become responsive to the individual.

CAVES, CAMPFIRES, WATERING HOLES

We know that humans need different learning environments to accomplish what they set out to learn: knowledge, competencies, and skills across the curriculum. That curriculum in ancient times was mostly about survival—how to farm, make tools, hunt, gather food, and so on. Humans learned using the early walls of caves, around the campfires of storytellers, and while exchanging goods and information with others who gathered with them at watering holes.

Young people watched master builders, hunters, and cooks in their tribes and villages, and they grew up learning through adult models, play, coaching, and eventually apprenticeships. They had access to a variety of teachers, aspirational peers, and environments in which to learn.

In the nineteenth century, when attending school to learn the basics of reading, writing, and math became an expectation for most children, the early ways of learning were abandoned in order to create environments of compliance, command, and control. Schools were set up with an intended outcome of learners gaining skills less to think creatively and critically to solve problems and more to follow directions. This shifted learning to a goal of developing compliant workers capable of replicating tasks over and over again.

The places of learning (schools) became cookie-cutter environments—classrooms with desks aligned in rows, a dominant teaching wall, access to the same resources that everyone used in the same way, and places where teacher talk dominated and student talk was minimized. The village learning model had evolved from children at the center of contextualized learning in their communities to children as recipients of teaching in schools. In that time, the purpose of learning changed the environments of acquisition.

However, given social, cultural, and technological changes in homes, communities, and the workforce of our states, nation, and around the globe, old paradigms of schools no longer are responsive to the needs of learners in today's world. That's why we need to reimagine and change learning spaces in ways that take us "back to the future" of engagement that comes from application and empowerment learning.

BACK TO THE FUTURE: HOW DO WE CHANGE CLASSROOM SPACES TO INCREASE ENGAGEMENT?

First, we must not just look inside schools to determine the changes needed. We must look to brain research that informs our understanding of how children learn from preschool to young adulthood. To learn, the body must move and the mind must sustain attention. Together, when students are designing, creating, building, engineering, and making learning through multiple modalities, they are more likely to feel a sense of agency and empowerment as learners.

Choice and comfort is a critical learning theme in our work, and the flexibility to sit, stand, or even gather on the floor is basic to students gaining autonomy within the physical environment as prerequisite to developing agency through self-directedness in the learning environment. Learners need access to natural light to the greatest degree possible and movement to sustain the brain's attention. This means uncovering and unblocking windows and using pedagogies that shift routinely to create experiential and interactive learning work (Barrett et al. 2015).

In some classrooms, we've seen children use cabinetry as window seats, as quiet reading or tech work spaces. Teachers have learned to create informal work spaces for children in front of windows, adding soft lamp lighting as an alternative to the factory glare of fluorescent overhead lighting. Teachers have in many cases abandoned their own desks in lieu of using joint work spaces alongside their learners.

Often, teachers create cave spaces for individuals to work alone using soft-seating chairs, couches, small tenting, and even using pillows underneath tables. Round tables are often sought after among teachers who understand the importance of campfire spaces for small-group work. Teachers can provide large area rugs to change spaces that accommodate whole-group gathering activities including short bursts of direct instruction or read-alouds.

The combination of formal and informal classroom environments offer the teacher and learners flexible informal and formal learning options throughout the day. We are learning that when students and teachers move routinely (Griss 2013), static teaching decreases, learner engagement increases, and classroom management issues decrease (*Movement Matters* 2015). Most importantly, the impact of movement on cognitive function leads to higher levels of performance (Jensen 2005). These changes in class learning spaces have been implemented in elementary, middle, and high school environments.

OUTSIDE THE CLASSROOM LEARNING SPACES: CHANGE THE OPPORTUNITIES

We underutilize the spaces available outside of classrooms as options for formal and informal learning. No space seems to be any more desirable to learners than working in hallways. An assistant superintendent once said, "When teachers and principals talk about the best learning activities kids have been doing, they are often happening out in the hall."

To gain more spaces for learning in a school, teachers do have to move to a place where they can trust learners to use those spaces in isolation from the teacher. One option is to remove lockers and replace them with benches, charging bars, and even whiteboards for group project design work.

In elementary and middle schools, any hallway nook or cranny can be used to place a small table or "sit-upon" in informal gathering spaces so children can move into halls and sprawl on the floor to work, read books, or create and then display projects. In one school, a physical education teacher has also adapted a seldom-used hallway to add fitness circuit activities using mobile equipment. Hallways offer huge square footage for small-group or individual work.

Teachers and principals have also changed cafeterias from institutional seating to family-style and cafe seating by going to round tables and higher and lower seating options that accommodate children sitting in different-sized groups. These choices also have shifted cafeterias from being used almost singularly for eating lunch to being used more as watering hole areas for multiple classes to gather and work together, sometimes content or grade based, but increasingly for multiage project work.

We also notice that learners gathered around a table talk more softly, with more people, and about different topics. They are learning pro-social skills and how to interact appropriately when not controlled by the schedule, the activity, and the teacher. Social-emotional learning gets practiced in spaces outside of structured classes as well as inside a classroom.

A school staff that also is interested in how to maximize the school library, a space that is increasingly questioned as a viable structure in schools, can find there is often *more* space in a library than meets the eye if multiple uses are envisioned. For example, our libraries from elementary to high schools have reduced storage needs by weeding collections, abandoning obsolete equipment and resources, and thinking about project work that kids could accomplish in the library with the librarian, the teacher, or on their own.

It's difficult to discard educational resources in a library, since the librarian never knows when one person will want that one very old book, cassette tape, or projector. But if we don't commit to "spring cleaning" and using every space for contemporary learning, we shortchange our kids. When librarians have weeded and tossed and envisioned what's possible, changing spaces becomes easier.

Across schools, librarians' offices have become a sound studio for kids to create music, videos, or podcasts. Old storage rooms have become design labs. Extra classrooms near the libraries may be makerspaces. The old "thousand-year-old" library furniture can be replaced with lightweight movable whiteboard tables, flex seating, and bookcases on casters. Try offering writable walls and multiple informal small gathering spaces for quiet reading, study groups, or project work.

The changes that have been made to shift to student-centered learning commons have caused our librarians to rethink every structure to better facilitate student uses of a variety of spaces. The circulation desks have been cut down in size and redeveloped as student-run help desks. The pedagogy of the library has shifted to the pedagogy of the learning commons and book circulation is up, more classes come to work on project research and development, lunchtime has become an opportunity for slam poets and musicians to perform, and students may be found sewing or hot-gluing or 3D-printing in library makerspaces ("Active Learning in the K12 School Library" 2016).

These changes are specific to our learning commons, but we see librarians in schools all over the country reimagining libraries that bring the world into the school, offering students a continuum of paths to search, connect, make, and communicate as they learn to seek resources and work on projects of importance to them.

Lastly, formal and informal environments can shift through do-it-yourself project work by kids and teachers or through more formal processes. For example, consider the school gym. When given the opportunity to upgrade fitness facilities, why not consider fitness center spaces instead of gyms? Today, we see fitness equipment, donated and purchased, in our classrooms, libraries, and lobbies.

In schools in our district, an observer may find students using fitness equipment *and* reading while pedaling or walking on treadmills. In lieu of building a new gym to respond to increased enrollment in one of the district's middle schools, fitness teachers on the design team made a proposal that resulted in building a fitness center with an indoor soccer, yoga, and dance space; a workout and strengthening area; and a cardiovascular center for less cost than an additional gym. Kids in this school now love going to fitness time because they can differentiate their wellness goals and make choices about activities each day.

Finally, there's the outdoor world of play areas, gathering spaces, and natural environments around schools. How might a staff work together to plan for routine use of such spaces? One school we know built a "water and mud" space for elementary play. Yes, you do have to tell parents to dress kids for messy time when you encourage kids to work outside, but the benefits of outdoor activity at recess and throughout the day lead to children who are learning social-emotional competencies "on the job" and applying learning in different ways.

Whether it's taking kids out during physics to build catapults and test force and motion formulas or to explore bee and butterfly gardens, when kids work outdoors on projects, they are motivated differently than in traditional learning work. Whether it's adding beehives for environmental science study or building chicken coops for a courtyard study of chickens, the grounds around a school offer opportunities for everything from ten-minute field trips to more intensive yearlong studies and just plain downtime for play or where teens can gather to eat lunch outside.

LEARNING IS EVERYWHERE—NOT JUST SCHOOL

Learning spaces are everywhere, inside and outside of schools as well as at home and in the community. Educators of contemporary learners have to consider the experiences that today's young people need to find success as students, regardless of demographic.

For example, home should not be a continuation of school, and the research on the disadvantages of traditional homework assignments is clear: the effect of size of homework shows it can actually work against motivating learning or add value as a learning path ("Why Homework Is Bad: Stress and Consequences" 2014). Homework that moves from worksheets to learning to cook a favorite recipe to interviewing family members about their memories for a podcast project creates a very different at-home learning space and reasons for communication for children.

School grounds can become learning spaces for project work and social engagement. Libraries, cafeterias, hallways, and gyms all hold opportunities to contextualize, integrate, and apply content learning and to practice working alone and self-directed competencies. For example, students can use math everywhere, participating in activities from timing their heartbeat before and after exercise, to cooking projects staged in the cafeteria, or figuring out what the most popular books are in the library.

Virtual learning spaces offer connectivity to the world beyond the walls of the school and the nation's boundaries as learners Skype with experts, engage in projects with classes in other states and nations, or go to YouTube to research or find out how to do a task they want to learn.

Beyond school, we must consider that we are part of communities of learners where students can explore and learn together beyond the school. When students get opportunities to do field research, not field trips, it means they begin to visit and even intern in businesses or local nonprofits, to work together on projects in coffee shops, and use their local libraries as resource spaces. In making these spaces not just available, but supported as learning spaces, we teach young people that learning is not limited to what they do in school.

CHANGING SPACE LEADERSHIP: WHAT WE CAN DO

Our children are part of a vast learning network today where the tools have expanded, the pedagogies needed to learn for this century are shifting, and the ways educators assess must become more about what kids can do and how they learn best than what they must memorize for a test. Learning spaces must change to accommodate social networked learning opportunities.

Leaders support change by encouraging teachers to try out new ideas for choice and comfort. Investing some school "seed" funds in innovations such as virtual reality (VR) tech tools to add to the suite of options for kids to explore other geographic regions or cultures. Asking for donations from the community can give teachers options to try out new ideas in their classrooms, the library, and halls.

Beginning to test innovation learning approaches with teachers who are willing to take small risks with change is a good way to get new models into the school. Supporting teachers to create a STEAM lab mobile cart encourages innovative thinking about what's possible and how to make innovation work accessible to all classrooms.

To make these kinds of changes, leaders must reexamine how they use staff meetings and staff time to shift to more focus on engagement of staff in professional learning about contemporary pedagogies and assessment. Principals must actively encourage teachers to start with small changes, giving teachers opportunities to watch students, make changes in practice, and test out new configurations of space.

Teachers can make observation visits to other classrooms that are making space changes, discuss what makes sense as differentiated space for learning in professional learning community meetings, and use those conversations to spark space redesign for kids who are experiencing difficulties in class. Creating a school Google site where teachers can share resources they are using to research and develop flexible learning spaces can offer access to more autonomous learning about changing space and why kids can benefit from those changes.

There is no one pathway to changing spaces, but all change begins with one step. Consider what you can change tomorrow. It may be as simple as cleaning books and stacks of papers from in front of a window or putting out a few materials in a creation station that are available for ongoing maker and project work. Teachers are making these changes in spite of leaders who don't see purpose or take the time to support them. But when leaders lead up for changing space, those changes can go viral in their schools.

WORKS CITED

"Active Learning in the K12 School Library." 2016. BCWH. February 8, 2016. http://bcwh.com/active-learning-in-the-k12-school-library/.

Barrett, Peter, Fay Davies, Yufan Zhang, and Lucinda Barrett. 2015. "The Impact of Classroom Design on Pupils' Learning: Final Results of a Holistic, Multi-level Analysis." *Building and Environment* 89 (July): 118–33.

Griss, Susan. 2013. "The Power of Movement in Teaching and Learning." *Education Week Teacher*, March 20, 2013. https://www.edweek.org/tm/articles/2013/03/19/tp_griss.html.

Jensen, Eric. 2005. "Movement and Learning." In *Teaching with the Brain in Mind*. Alexandria, VA: ASCD. http://www.ascd.org/publications/books/104013/chapters/movement-and-learning.aspx.

Movement Matters. 2015. Trinity College of Dublin: National Behaviour Support Service. https://www.nbss.ie/sites/default/files/publications/movement_matters_report.pdf.

"Why Homework Is Bad: Stress and Consequences." 2014. Healthline. March 11, 2014. https://www.healthline.com/health-news/children-more-homework-means-more-stress-031114.

Chapter Nine

Financial Awareness

An investment in knowledge pays the best interest.—Benjamin Franklin

QUESTIONS TO PONDER IN THIS CHAPTER

- *In what ways does funding help move a vision for learning into reality?*
- *How might staff be involved in the process of determining needed changes and prioritizing those for funding?*
- *How can a building leader leverage funding for specific projects?*
- *What do you think are the most important parts of the design and funding processes and why?*

FUNDING PHILOSOPHY

How school staff and administrators make decisions about and use a variety of resource funds determines whether a school community is able to advance its work to become contemporary in practices, tool options, and space design. All are essential if learners are to receive the kind of experiential opportunities that make a difference in their success now and in the future.

At their best, funding decisions are made and shared transparently within the school community. After all, people do notice where funds are used, whether for textbooks or new chairs in the office. Of course, use of funds should be aligned with the school's vision and philosophy for learning. For example, using professional development funds to send a teacher team to an in-depth workshop on project-based learning aligns teacher planning and student work with a vision focus on student engagement.

In fact, without a shared vision for learning, funds may get used in random ways and simply reinforce the maxim "If you always do what you

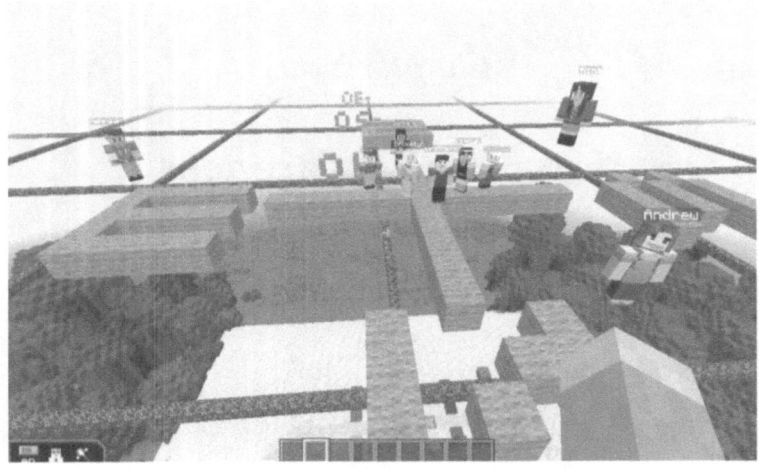

always did, you will get what you always got." This can occur when a principal goes to a conference and is wowed by a software package that drills procedural math when school data suggest that learners need to develop deep conceptual understanding of math. Without a shared vision, decisions get made that change little at the classroom level. Reenvisioning the way resources are used and the processes for determining use is an imperative for change to occur and for the school's vision for learning to be realized.

THE PROCESS

Effective use of school funds, regardless of source, begins with philosophical questions. What's the vision behind the process? Who makes the decision? Who gives input? How does allocation and use of resources align with the vision? Does everyone know the process for using funds? What data and information might inform the process? How do decisions get communicated? Most importantly, when faced with choices of funding one need over another, why does one get funding and the other doesn't?

School principals have a continuum of funding streams over which they may exert little, some, or full control over. Funds may come from non–school board sources such as grants, partnerships, parent organizations, and even activities of clubs or school groups that donate money to improve the school. In addition, school principals may have discretionary funds in a board-determined operational budget. Finally, principals have access to in-kind funding that may include donations or people power to accomplish specific tasks that will help the school.

Financial Awareness 93

If your school philosophy and vision align with and support contemporary learning, then your funds must be refocused to support different work by learners. Most educators would describe contemporary schooling as students learning to do the following:

- Create unique projects and products that demonstrate deep learning knowledge and skills
- Think critically within and across content areas
- Communicate in a variety of forms of media
- Work well with team members to accomplish goals together
- Work actively in their community to improve the quality of life for self and others

A leader who works to align strategic goals with school funding will want to use a defined process to engage teachers in robust strategic planning that purposefully develops their knowledge capacity to determine gaps that must be addressed with funds and practices that will do so. That process begins with keeping the vision and expected outcomes actively in front of staff as a focus for funding decisions that realize work toward the vision. These steps outline a focus for process work:

1. The leader both models for and encourages staff to seek and share well-vetted research on best practices aligned with a shared vision for learning.
2. Staff analyzes and uses learning data, observations, and information to inform decisions.
3. Design teams form with an intention to discover how to make learner experiences engaging, empowering, and student owned. This means engaging with learners to find out what they value individually and as groups.
4. Whenever possible, design teams visit other sites that are known for innovative learning—both virtual and face-to-face trips help to expand ideas.
5. Opportunities to test out new classroom designs are built into the change process with teachers who are confident in the change process.
6. Professional development is planned and implemented to build capacity of staff to use new learning environments that promote active learners, team interaction, project-based and maker learning opportunities, choice and comfort, and use of interactive and connected learning tools.
7. Teachers, and even learners, have the chance to share input about proposed changes. For example, giving students the opportunity to try

out new devices or flexible seating provides staff with insights into student perspectives.
8. Final decisions are shared with staff, along with all the research and rationale, for making those decisions and the funds to support implementation.

EMPATHY IS KEY TO THE PROCESS

The design thinking process is key to making funding decisions that will influence future directions for learning. Without a focus on the intentional end in mind of changes in practice and expectations for what and how children will learn, then school staff function more like "independent contractors" and less like a learning community with shared values, beliefs, and practices.

One area of the design process is particularly important to determining what changes in environment will serve learners well. It's easy to find good tools for design work. The free IDEO *Design Thinking for Educators Toolkit* offers one path to making decisions from a position of empathetic response (IDEO 2012) about redesigning learning spaces and environments for learners. In that process, the most important stage is interviewing users, in this case learners, about the experiences that delight them, brings joy, creates enthusiasm, and empowers them.

Through this process, the interviewer's *empathic* response to the learner opens more and more doors to understand the interviewee's hopes and dreams, frustrations, and values and beliefs about their school experiences.

This means all students should have the opportunity to talk with an adult about what matters to them as learners. In seeking out feedback from learners, adults should focus on empathizing with the learner, exhibiting a sincere interest in listening to feedback, asking reflective questions such as "When do you find yourself doing your best work?" then taking notes for use in informing the team's decision-making process.

FINANCIAL CONSIDERATIONS

School funding does come from a variety of sources. In making decisions about the use of funds, the effective leader knows how to prioritize the use of funds for new tools, furnishings, and learning resources and when and how to stop funding that is no longer consistent with the learning vision.

Sometimes purchases—from printer cartridges for printers no longer in use to too much paper for too many worksheets—become so routine that no one even questions them, while some funds might not get expended at all and result in a balance of unused funds at the end of the year. A good assessment of purchases and data on usage helps a school to redirect funds to new needs that emerge in a redesign process. With the technologies available today, it's far easier to collect this information in a database and use it during the budget review process. Knowing how projected and actual expenditures balance is key to knowing how funds are being expended and used.

Secondly, when a school staff invests in the decision to try out new tools, resources, or even furnishings, it's important to bring parent organizations and community partners into the plan. They often may be sources of funding for the design plan that staff members have created. If multiple funding sources can be blended, this helps advance the vision for change faster than when purchases are dependent upon the school alone.

Sometimes new space designs, for example, a library makerspace, can be furnished and funded for next to nothing by making a wish list of needs and seeking donations from sewing machines to glue guns to cardboard or scrap lumber. You don't have to start with thousands of dollars of high-end tech equipment to establish a makerspace. Teachers also may be able to work with the parent organization to request donations of comfortable couches, bean-bags, and other soft seating to add into classrooms for learners' use.

Many teachers today are using social media donor sites such as Donors-Choose.org to share their needs, and they can sometimes obtain relatively expensive equipment, books, or other resources by describing their needs. This has been especially effective for some teachers in at-risk schools who have had books or sophisticated equipment such as 3D printers donated to diversify class libraries. However, teachers need to work with the principal and even school tech support to ensure that technology will be functional and supported if funded through a donation site.

Finally, principals must prioritize how to purchase those resources that may start with small test bed pilot projects and assessments of impact. If STEM resources are a priority, looking for good-quality tools and consumables that can be tried out in a few classrooms helps to prevent sinking significant funds into a redesign project before learners have had a chance to use the resources and teachers have had the chance to learn how to set up STEM activities in the classroom.

Without professional development on using redesigned new tools, teachers often continue to teach as they always did and students don't benefit from the changing resources, but both likely will use tools inappropriately, "proving" that the changes don't work.

An effective school leader constantly researches and shares this with staff on new tools and resources, whether laser cutters or a particular tech platform that could advance student project work. This school leader will participate in social media to find out where others are already engaging in innovation of space design or use of technologies such as virtual reality.

In figuring out what steps to take to bring new resources and design ideas into a school community, the effective school leader also knows who in central office can add support through grant writing, leveraging operational or capital resources. In making those connections, the building leader must be able to coherently articulate a plan incorporating the school's vision, goals, priorities, and metrics for using resources differently.

This increases the likelihood of securing additional resources to make changes in practice and environmental and resource use. The effective leader knows how to budget his or her own discretionary funding so that purchases can be made quickly from staff priority lists as sales on items may make a tool accessible that otherwise would be out of reach.

SEED FUNDING

The use of seed funding for special projects also is in the list of ideas that effective leaders use to promote change in schools. This means setting aside what may be a small amount of school budget funds that can be accessed by staff who have an idea what they would like to try out in the classroom, library, gym, or hallway. Funding innovation is a must in private, for-profit businesses (Power and Stanton 2014), but school funding often is set up to focus on operational and even strategic needs, but not necessarily for innovation funding. Setting aside funding to support innovative ideas from educators to try out an approach designed to support the vision of the school can make a real difference in a school community's effort to expand its potential to impact learning.

Often a short proposal format might be used to elicit seed project ideas. We try to keep these proposals simple:

1. Describe what you plan to do in 300 words or less.
2. Make a list of the resources you need to implement your plan with itemized costs for each.
3. What are the outcomes you have identified for students to accomplish as a result of engaging in the project?
4. How will students share what they have accomplished with an authentic audience?
5. In what ways will you share your project after completion with others in the district?

For example, a teacher team might want to add standing desks or an exercise bike for use by students who have higher than typical activity levels whether with a medical diagnosis or not. These funds could be used to add an idea wall in the library for students to do design work or plan out projects.

Or, they could support purchase of a particular technology that can be shared in a maker area of the school, such as a laser cutter.

These funds, however, should be accessible to any teacher and be awarded, perhaps by the design team, to promote vision work for the school. These funds help to create test bed projects around the school that allow other teachers to see how learning is impacted that's consistent with expectations. Information about seed projects should be collected and shared with staff.

FINANCIAL AWARENESS

Funding is a driver of change and a driver of status quo in schools. Decisions that are made mindlessly and without alignment with the school's vision often result in status quo maintenance. However, when staff become a part of the process, researching, sharing input, and designing, then they are more likely as a team to develop social cohesion, collective efficacy, and common purpose in choosing resources and environmental design options that support all learners to be active, engaged, and empowered.

This happens when school staff are afforded autonomy in the use of funds to address differentiated needs and ideas for addressing those rather than the one-size-fits-all funding approaches usually associated with top-down management (Rainwater 2016).

When learners are invited into the process through interviews or surveys to share their perspectives, staff start to notice that students bring perspective to the "table" that informs their own thinking. For example, you might invite young children to play with several different device tablets you are considering for purchase and ask them which one they liked best and why.

While a teacher might prefer the larger-sized tablet, students may favor the smaller ones for ease of use. Engaging students in the process makes the teachers' recommendation easier and more responsive to the learners they serve.

Taking the time to deeply study, engage stakeholders, and test-bed ideas for change may slow down the process, but in the long run better decisions will be made through collective input processes than when a leader works alone to determine funding priorities and decisions.

WORKS CITED

IDEO. 2012. *Design Thinking for Educators Toolkit.* IDEO.94 pages. https://designthinkingforeducators.com/toolkit/.

Power, Brad, and Steve Stanton. 2014. "How to Prioritize Your Innovation Budget." *Harvard Business Review*, September 24, 2014. https://hbr.org/2014/09/how-to-prioritize-your-innovation-budget.

Rainwater, Kendi A. 2016. "Nashville Educators Share Approach to School Funding with Hamilton County." 2016. *Chattanooga (TN) Times Free Press*, June 9, 2016. http://www.timesfreepress.com/news/local/story/2016/jun/09/nasvhille-educators-share-approach-school-fun/370151/.

Chapter Ten

Radical Leadership

Leadership is an ever-evolving position.—Mike Krzyzewski

QUESTIONS TO PONDER IN THIS CHAPTER

- *In what ways can school leaders set up change to make a difference with kids who aren't successful?*
- *How might a school leader assess the need for change?*
- *What does autonomy mean in the context of school? Can schools be autonomous?*
- *What do you see as the critical competencies of leadership and why?*
- *In what ways can central office leaders from the superintendent on down better support school change leadership?*

LEADERSHIP BASICS

School leaders must be in touch with the communities they serve. This doesn't happen in isolation but with interaction and engagement with people. Most school administrators of the past century were trained and hired to manage and evaluate budgets, schedules, resources, disciplinary actions, facilities, and staff. They were expected to make schools "run on time." As the workforce and society changed in the 1990s, the role of the school administrator was redefined as change leader, not just status quo manager (Fullan 2002).

This change in scope of what school leaders do represents a sea change in the competencies required to effectively meet the needs of increasingly diverse learners, beginning with supporting educators to understand why changes are needed, what changes will have the greatest impact, and how to make those changes. It also means that school leaders must build relationships with staff, parents, community members, and learners who with leaders will network, seek ideas, research, and communicate across the boundaries of roles as opportunities for needed change are identified.

Nothing changes in schools unless staff embrace new practices and let those practices through a school's doors (Dintersmith 2018). The competent leader works from a three-pronged philosophy that builds individual and collective efficacy for change (Donohoo 2016):

1. People are motivated to change when they understand the need and believe they can make a difference.
2. Readiness for change begins by understanding that people need differentiated paths, time, and resources to engage in deep change.
3. Owning goals for change is everybody's business for collective efficacy to grow.

Understanding how people learn is a prerequisite to radical leadership for change.

Accepting that change will not happen on their own timetable is a hallmark of leaders who work well with staff to effect change. Being the kind of leader who can articulate a vision for why radical change is needed is key.

RADICAL LEADERSHIP

"How might we _____?" is the key question of design thinkers ("'How Might We' Questions," n.d.). Radical leaders, at the heart of their work, are designers who know how to engage teams alongside them in the creative work of change. They are willing to give up positional power as they empower others to lead with them. They understand that social-emotional competencies—empathy, kindness, collaboration, listening, reflecting, conversing—are at the heart of leading for radical shifts in how staff come to value change as it relates to maximizing their own potential in working with learners.

Radical school leaders deeply study their own organizations, spend time observing and noticing the capabilities of others around them, and metacognitively reflect upon their own thinking as they lead (Witmer, n.d.). For example, such leaders spend time walking their school daily, observing in classrooms and stopping in classes, the cafeteria, and the lounge to chat with staff and students.

Such leaders listen carefully and make notes of themes they hear. They know their school's data and have analyzed trend lines and shared those with the staff. They give educators opportunities to take on projects associated with strategic work in the school, and when creating teams, they focus on how to create ones that are diverse across multiple variables. Radical leaders look outside themselves for critical friends with whom they can reflect on areas that are a challenge as well as progress on goals they have set. They keep a journal and make notes on their observations, resources, and feedback.

Such school leaders make sense of context, and as they grow their own skills, they come to intuit what will move individuals to make changes. They embrace that a diversity of ideas emerges and builds change efforts by intersecting teams with different demographics and experiences (Johansson 2017). Just as school leaders value the autonomy afforded them in a site-based district culture, they afford that to school staff as well. This means shifting power from the principal's office chair to the school community.

HOW DO SCHOOL LEADERS DO THAT?

They walk schools daily, looking for opportunities to interact with teachers, parents, and learners. They note on their cell phones what they notice and even use social media to share images, videos, and success stories aligned with and reinforcing of the school's vision and mission work. The purpose of their daily walks is not to evaluate, but to build relationships and offer support. They also bring their community into learning walks as a tool to learn and support development of practices across the school (Gaddis 2016).

Radical leaders give away power in a variety of ways. They rely on staff as partners in developing and implementing professional learning. In radically led schools, it's more usual to see teachers running staff meetings than the principal, not as business meetings but as opportunities to engage and interact around research and strategies essential to keeping children at the center of decisions and actions of the staff.

In such meetings, whether small or large group, staff talk about what matters. For example, teachers might read a shared text or study differentiated resources on critical topics of change. They might have noticed that many kids reported being disinterested in their work on a student survey and now are digging in, through staff meetings, to try out and share practices such as PBLs that increase engagement. They engage teacher leaders to figure out how teams or departments can take on this work so that it isn't reserved for the principal.

Or they may research how to implement student-led conferences within a study team. They may share their work and invite peers to observe them. This kind of work can happen in spite of administrators, but when it happens because of them, the empowerment of the community grows exponentially.

Radical leaders also challenge beliefs and values that are inconsistent with equity, access, and opportunity for all learners. Quality work is dependent upon perspective. Radical leaders help staff develop operational definitions and images of what it means for all learners to engage in quality work ("Engaging Students in Learning," n.d.). They ask critical questions such as "How do you know learners aren't bored in your classes?" that leads to dissonance in the thinking of others.

They value themselves being pushed to consider different points of view. They also understand that running a school "happiness club" isn't their job because challenging staff to learn can be uncomfortable. At the same time, they think about what individual staff need to develop the capability to take risks to try new practices, to even fail with those, and continue to evolve or iterate toward success. They serve as both cheerleader and coach. They know the best solutions come from the collective intelligence of the team, not just one person.

Finally, radical leaders are seekers. They never accept that they "are there," for they know that as long as even one learner isn't reaching their potential or on a path to reach their hopes and dreams, their work isn't finished. They read books and blogs, watch videos, talk with peers, Skype, visit those who are innovating beyond them, and study recent impact research to scour opportunities for new ways of approaching learning.

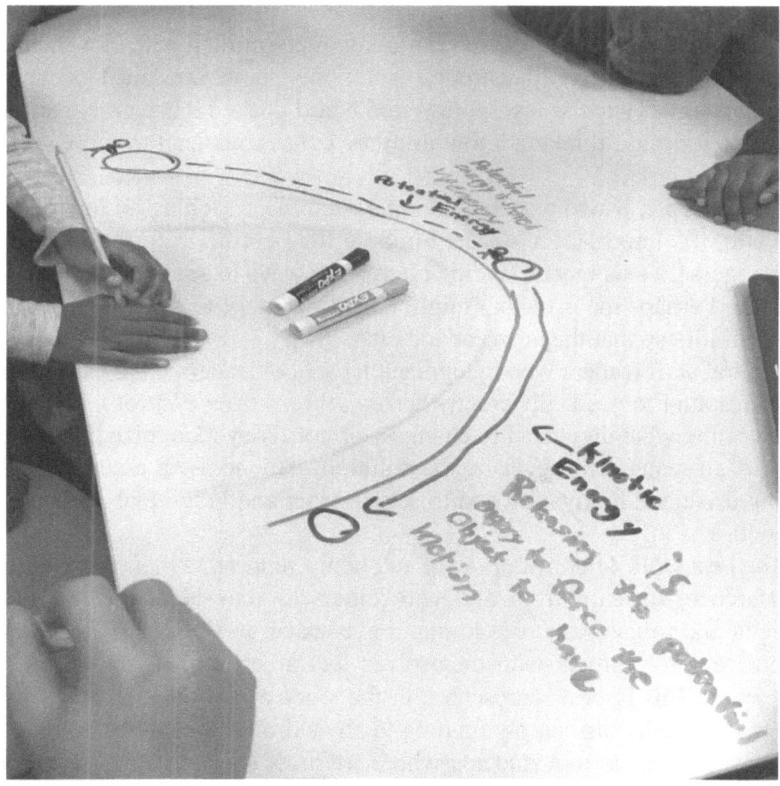

They also stay true to a vision that learners must believe their voice is of value, their agency matters, and they can have influence for good in their school and community. This they know is the foundation for child-centered decisions, and they constantly connect people with each other, resources, and ideas for radically improving their communities.

Ultimately, the most radical leaders are connectors, communicators, and creative and critical thinkers. They do not accept "no" to great ideas from their school. They themselves get to "yes" on great ideas from staff, students, and parents (Vander Ark 2018). They do that by figuring out how to work with others to shape ideas to ensure that innovative projects are grounded in safe practices and have a learning goal consistent with the school's vision in mind. If funding is a challenge, they work on alternatives that sustain the essence of a project. They may work with the teacher who proposed a project to scale down its scope. They are not afraid to take risks. They are "what if," not "yeah . . . but" participants in the work of making schools exciting, joyful, and engaging learning communities.

Chapter 10

AUTONOMY

Autonomy is key to each school community determining paths for their own journey to success for all learners. Autonomy, however, must occur with some constraints such as law, policy, and board goals. However, experienced educational design thinkers know minimal constraints lead to more creative solutions.

For example, if two teachers are interested in coteaching an interdisciplinary unit, it's important to not let limits of time constrain their capability to work together. This means finding alternative ways to support them working together. Perhaps the principal might take lunch duty to free them from that responsibility so that they can eat and plan.

Central staff leaders who recognize that school leaders must have autonomy to respond to needs differently across schools offer control to the school to determine what they need to change—or not. They recognize that the one-size-fits-all result will never be the solution. Autonomy is essential to sustaining drive and motivation and to setting team and individual goals consistent with vision.

The best work of educators with autonomy represents their drive to make a difference, to learn from and with others as they meet challenges and barriers, and to use resources to maximize success. Autonomy aligned with vision leads to learners who themselves feel a sense of autonomy in their own work. This is best represented in the story of two elementary teachers who pooled their class supply funding to buy a drone (McCombs, n.d.).

They then asked two students who were most excited about the drone to learn how to use it and then teach other kids. Before long, the two "drone pilots" were signing up classmates for group and private lessons. They began teaching peers to capture video, fly, and land the drone. Empowered? Yes! Self-directed? Absolutely!

It's what the best leaders do as they shift from sustaining traditions for the sake of traditions to figuring out how to target areas of learning work that demand a new way of thinking. That's the essence of what radical change leaders do whether teacher, principal, or central office leader.

WORKS CITED

Dintersmith, Ted. 2018. *What School Could Be: Insights and Inspiration from Teachers across America*. Princeton, NJ: Princeton University Press.

Donohoo, Jenni. 2016. *Collective Efficacy: How Educators' Beliefs Impact Student Learning*. Thousand Oaks, CA: Corwin.

"Engaging Students in Learning." n.d. University of Washington, Center for Teaching and Learning. Accessed July 8, 2018. https://www.washington.edu/teaching/teaching-resources/engaging-students-in-learning/.

Fullan, Michael. 2002. "The Change Leader." *Educational Leadership* 59, no 8 (May 2002): 16–21. http://www.ascd.org/publications/educational-leadership/may02/vol59/num08/The-Change-Leader.aspx.

Gaddis, Hillary. 2016. "Lit. Review Reflection: Using Teacher Learning Walks to Improve Instruction (Fisher & Frey, 2014)." Hillary Gaddis, Educator. July 7, 2016. http://hillarygaddis.weebly.com/20-project-blog/lit-review-reflection-using-teacher-learning-walks-to-improve-instruction-fisher-frey-2014.

"'How Might We' Questions." n.d. Stanford d.school. Accessed July 8, 2018. https://dschool.stanford.edu/resources/how-might-we-questions.

Johansson, Frans. 2017. *The Medici Effect, with a New Preface and Discussion Guide: What Elephants and Epidemics Can Teach Us about Innovation*. Boston: Harvard Business Review Press.

McCombs, Barbara. n.d. "Developing Responsible and Autonomous Learners: A Key to Motivating Students." American Psychological Association. Accessed July 8, 2018. http://www.apa.org/education/k12/learners.aspx.

Vander Ark, Tom. 2018. "Find a Way to Yes: Leadership Lessons from School Superintendent Pam Moran."*Forbes Magazine*, May 30, 2018. https://www.forbes.com/sites/tomvanderark/2018/05/30/find-a-way-to-yes-leadership-lessons-from-pam-moran/.

Witmer, Adam. n.d. "Radical Leadership: The 4 R's of a Radical Leader." *Adam Witmer* (blog). Accessed July 8, 2018. https://www.adamwitmer.com/blog/radical-leadership.

Chapter Eleven

Decision-Making

Choice and Comfort

> *Excellence is never an accident. It is always the result of high intention, sincere effort and intelligent execution; it represents the wise choice of many alternatives—choice, not chance, determines your destiny.*—Aristotle

QUESTIONS TO PONDER IN THIS CHAPTER

- *How can teachers give students more academic choice in the classroom?*
- *How does student choice lead to a space for risk?*
- *Why does comfort matter in the classroom?*
- *How do choice and comfort relate to each other in the learning space?*

WHY CHOICE AND COMFORT?

Choice and comfort are two of the most valuable components of the twenty-first-century classroom. Students need to feel they have a voice in the classroom. They also need the opportunity to be comfortable while they learn and grow. This might seem obvious, but choice and comfort in the classroom have been ignored for many years. Not all students learn in the same way. Offering academic choice and a comfortable learning atmosphere could inevitably be the difference between some students succeeding in school while others fall short.

Allowing students a choice in the classroom and giving them a space that is comfortable and productive is not always easy. Even so, it is an imperative part of creating a space for risk. Developing a space for risk means that the students feel confident and comfortable in their surroundings. Their frame of mind will often dictate their willingness to work and take risks. If they are consistently uncomfortable, their work quality will suffer. Furthermore, if students feel decisions are always being dictated for them, they will likely begin to lose faith in their work and in the direction of the classroom.

It is educators' responsibility to understand the value of choice and comfort. From there, they should develop a space that honors the needs of their learners so that both the educator and the student can learn in the best possible situation. Then the focus can be on academia and critical thinking and less on individual student behaviors.

This happens when teachers use structures such as class meetings or daily individual conferences to set the stage for ongoing conversations with students about their learning needs and how the teacher can help them find success through more personal responses to individual learners. Personal responses mean differentiated activities, such as a "playlist" of choices that students can help construct.

ACADEMIC CHOICE

Students should be given the opportunity to make academic choices in the classroom. Typically, the curriculum is set with little to no input from the actual learner. Most likely this is not something that can be changed by an individual teacher. Even so, individual classroom teachers can have a vital impact on the opportunities that students have within the realm of the set curriculum. For this to happen, teachers will have to be willing to relinquish some control of the classroom so that students have more space to learn and grow.

What is academic choice? At its core, academic choice is providing multiple learning opportunities in the classroom. It is an instructional pedagogy that will change based on the activities and projects in the classroom. There are many ways to increase academic choice in the classroom. Teachers can create choice with individual tasks such as which of the three assignments a student would complete. Choice of evaluation could be either an assessment or a project. Students can choose to do even problems or odd for math homework. The more options available to the students, the more effort they will put into the work.

Teachers should provide various academic options for students without limiting their opportunity to choose. For example, when setting up a unit on fact and opinion, students might use a variety of resources to explore what differentiates "fake news" from objective reporting of news. If the teacher uses a Socratic seminar approach to discussing a common reading, students might choose a second article they want to bring into the discussion.

In short, don't create a learning opportunity with multiple options and then undermine it by making the instructional decisions for the students. Instead, develop the initial framework for the project and then hand it over to the students.

They will fill in the holes with their creativity and ingenuity. Not every aspect of a lesson needs to be determined by the teacher. When teachers overplan a lesson, academic choice will be limited, and creativity and critical thinking could be limited as well.

It is not easy to abandon traditional instructional techniques by offering students more academic choices in the classroom. It will pull teachers more into the trenches of learning. One such way is to develop lessons that have more options during academic activities, providing students with either options of novels on a particular theme or different media to communicate what they have learned in the course of a unit. This simple change will enable more students the opportunity to discover a method that better suits them (Ronan et al. 2015).

Even when there is an established curriculum, the students can still determine how they are learning the information. The better option is to allow each student to dictate their own learning path in which they are able to put together every day some choices of what they will do to accomplish a learning target, such as "I can write an opinion blog post with an introduction, supporting details, and a conclusion." As teachers align vision, curriculum, and instructional activities, students make learning choices beginning in elementary school and continuing along through high school.

When students have more of a voice in their individual learning, they will also have more investment in the final product. This will lead to students creating instructional paths that would otherwise not have been available to them. The educator's job is to provide the platform that allows for that independence in the classroom. Instructional independence and academic choice will lead to more peer-to-peer collaboration, creativity, and critical thinking.

Furthermore, academic choice will lead to more student production. Students want to feel connected to the classroom and to the curriculum. For too long, there has been a separation between the students and the curriculum. The curriculum was fed to them in many ways using a variety of instructional methods. Regardless of the delivery, students were not involved in the development of the lesson.

In many classrooms, teachers write lesson plans, develop projects, and conduct activities while students are directed to complete whatever has been planned for them. Instead, teachers should step back and grant students more academic responsibility in the classroom, such as figuring out how to take charge of sharing technologies so that everyone gets access to tools they need or curating their own portfolios of best work. Increasing the instructional responsibility of the students will lead to more production because the students will have more stakes in the process and outcome.

Academic choice will also help students build more academic endurance. It is easy to abandon a project or assignment that is challenging when the assignment or project is assigned with little to no input from the learner. Contrarily, students who have invested time developing their own learning path will endure more to see it come to fruition. The curriculum is the same, but now the students will approach the information with a new set of eyes as they create and critically think about how the curriculum can be learned.

STUDENT CHOICE AND A SPACE FOR RISK

Having established the value of student choice in the classroom, it is now important to connect student choice to a space for risk. Just like adults, children need to feel safe. The feeling of safety will allow students to take more risks in the classroom. For example, a student who often chooses the easiest activities to complete may be encouraged to take on a more difficult project. The teacher promises that even if the activity isn't completed, taking the risk to work on harder work will be of value, especially since the student will have a chance to redo the work to fix errors without a grade penalty.

For grading to not contextualize high-stakes failures that set up students to go for the good grade and not for the learning, the teacher's instructional methodology must change in order for a space for risk to develop (Ingram 2017). When it comes to grading practices, the use of a mastery model moves students away from one-shot testing or assessments impacting their grade.

Risk taking is likely to happen in most classrooms. Children are not turned off by failure enough to always make the safe decision. Students see the classroom in a different light, and often their expectations of success versus failure are different. These are two attributes that every teacher should take advantage of when creating a learning space.

The learning space is not just the physical aspects of the classroom. It is also framed by the instructional design and pedagogical decisions of the instructional staff. To allow students the opportunity to make instructional decisions, we have ourselves had to learn to stop micromanaging the learning space. Micromanaged learning is detrimental to student success and especially detrimental to a space for risk (Linsin 2012).

Every instructional decision does not have to be made by the teacher. In fact, the goal for a space for risk is that the learners are making judgments and decisions independently. The teacher is there to guide their decision-making without sheltering them from taking risks or making mistakes. Students need the space to learn, mature, make mistakes, and problem solve.

Their independence will lead to more critical thinking and creativity, which will tie directly to academic performance.

THE COMFORTABLE CLASSROOM

The classroom should be an evolving space for learning. It should not look and feel the same on a day-to-day basis. It should be flexible so that the learners can use it as needed. Flexible furniture and equipment will open up the space to more student creativity. In addition to flexibility, it is imperative the space is comfortable. Flexibility and comfort together are two defining characteristics of a space for risk.

Comfort is subjective. One student might discover that a couch is an ideal learning spot while another might seek out a mat for the floor. Then the next

day their choice could change because of a new activity or lesson. Students can and should make these decisions based on their learning needs. These are not decisions that should be made by teachers for students. This is the exact type of micromanaging that will prohibit a space for risk from forming. Limiting these important decisions will also limit a student's faith in the direction of the classroom.

How can a space be comfortable for every student? Developing a comfortable classroom is a challenge for teachers and administrators. Comfort means from our perspective that students are able to use a restroom when needed, not on a teacher's timetable. Comfort also means not knowing the answers and being able to acknowledge the need for assistance from a peer or the teacher. Comfort is also being able to choose to not work with another person and being able to say that you need to be alone to work.

Furthermore, students should be able to navigate the learning space without feeling their every move is being watched and judged. Traditionally speaking, students typically get assigned a spot in the classroom. They are not allowed to move from their spot without permission from the teacher in the classroom. Eliminate this needless tradition and grant students the ability to choose their own learning space in the classroom. Allowing them this freedom will bring a sense of physical and emotional comfort to the classroom ("Flexible Seating Elevates Student Engagement" 2015).

Freedom to move throughout the classroom will help each student work well independently and collaboratively. Knowing the teachers have faith in them and their decisions will relieve a stress that persists in many classrooms. As their comfort level rises, their willingness to work harder will rise as well. In turn, their commitment to their classwork will lead to fewer behavioral issues. In the end, students will roam freely while learning on their own terms in a comfortable environment that fosters risk taking and decision-making.

A space for risk depends on many classroom and instructional elements. Comfort, both physical and mental, is paramount in the classroom. Urging students to fear less and fail more is not easy. It is especially hard when students are not physically and mentally comfortable in the learning space. Their comfort level will help foster their willingness to move past mistakes.

Children, like adults, want to work in a space that allows them to feel peaceful and comfortable. With comfort also comes a sense of tranquility that is important when people are asked to think critically. It is hard to focus and stay on task when there is concern with the environment. The lack of a comfortable environment will hinder the creative process and decrease a student's desire to work hard.

A space for risk requires full commitment from the students to work hard, stay on task, and think critically and creatively. If space is hindering this,

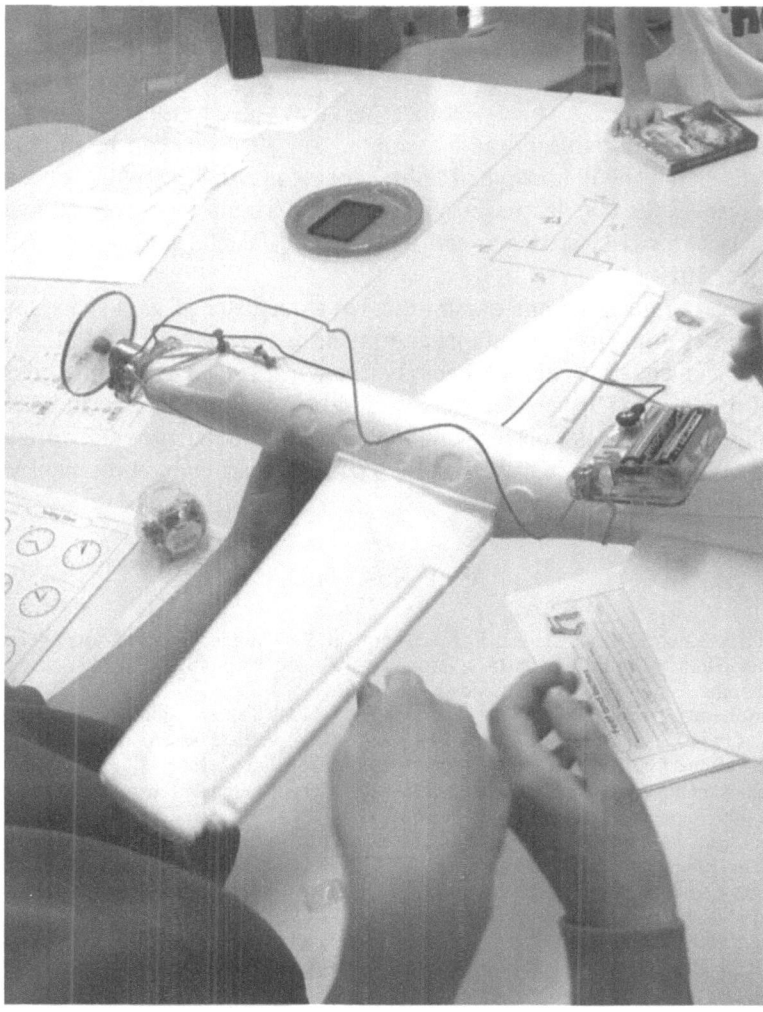

then the school is failing the students. Teachers and administrators must work together to improve the space so that more learning can happen.

If that means arranging the room differently or adding other options to the classroom, then that is what should happen. Some students like to listen to music while working; allowing headphones and the use of cell phones for music can provide students with a level of comfort that they do not feel if others are talking while they work. In the end, the goal is for every student to learn in the best way possible. Every student is different in their likes and dislikes, and therefore their choices will vary.

We have found differentiating to meet a variety of needs to be the greatest necessity we have as educators given that our goal is that every learner experience academic success, a sense of belonging, and that their voices matter to us.

Each student has a voice. Let them use that voice to articulate what they need to be comfortable in the classroom. Not all needs can be met, but at least the students will know their voice is being heard. They will also develop more respect for the classroom when they understand their opinion matters. In a space for risk, students lead and teachers listen, guide, and facilitate (Spencer 2018).

Instead of guessing and assuming what students need, in a space for risk teachers ask students and truly listen to their response. This level of communication can be hard. This is especially true when students are brutally honest about the learning space. Teachers should be open to criticism and develop an interdependent relationship with their students so that all voices are heard in the classroom. This will help build a positive learning environment where risk is more likely to happen.

WORKS CITED

"Flexible Seating Elevates Student Engagement." 2015. Edutopia. George Lucas Educational Foundation. April 8, 2015. https://www.edutopia.org/practice/flexible-classrooms-providing-learning-environment-kids-need.

Ingram, Leticia Guzman. 2017. "A Classroom Full of Risk Takers." Edutopia. George Lucas Educational Foundation. 2017. https://www.edutopia.org/article/classroom-full-risk-takers.

Linsin, Michael. 2012. "Why Micromanagers Make Bad Teachers." Smart Classroom Management. May 26, 2012. https://www.smartclassroommanagement.com/2012/05/26/why-micromanagers-make-bad-teachers/.

Ronan, Amanda, James Hinton, Don Kilburn, Edudemic Staff, Marian Oswald, George Jones, Adam Gutierrez, and Shawn McCusker. 2015. "7 Ways to Hack Your Classroom to Include Student Choice." Edudemic. March 20, 2015. http://www.edudemic.com/7-ways-to-hack-your-classroom/.

Spencer, John. 2018. "Who Owns the Learning in Your Classroom?" *John Spencer* (blog). May 1, 2018. http://www.spencerauthor.com/who-owns-the-learning-in-your-classroom/.

Chapter Twelve

The Learning Space and Student Autonomy in the Classroom

Everyone can rise above their circumstances and achieve success if they are dedicated to and passionate about what they do.—Mother Teresa

QUESTIONS TO PONDER IN THIS CHAPTER

- *Are your students allowed free movement with a purpose the majority of time in their classroom?*
- *Do you allow all students to be leaders in the classroom?*
- *Do your students feel ownership for their space and especially for their learning?*

SILENT MYSTERY WALK/GALLERY WALK

The sound of soft jazz plays in the room as seventh-grade students work on a lesson about irony. Moving around the room, looking at images illustrating the ironic, they work, laugh, and talk about what they are discussing at their choice of seating. They switch from full engagement to adolescent distraction, and back, as the teacher watches, observes, and occasionally intervenes. This is a scene of action, not that different in appearance than if the same students were observed outside the school during lunch. It's difficult at first to locate Cheryl, the teacher, until she laughs, as she is located among the students. Observing the class, it's obvious that students and the teacher share a collegial relationship.

To shift students into the irony activity, Cheryl posed three questions, shared via a Google Doc with the students:

1. What do you think these examples suggest?
2. What other item would you add? Why?
3. What concept do you think we are about to embark upon studying?

This activity is called a gallery walk and is one of many techniques Cheryl uses to observe students at work. Also known as a silent mystery walk, this takes approximately ten to fifteen minutes. (The word *silent* had to be added for those who enjoy discussing what they notice as they observe.) It is quite wonderful to see the "aha" moments, on student's faces, when they "get" what we are about to discuss even if they can't label it as irony—yet.

Some students have those moments quicker than others do, and that is why it is silent. This is a kickoff activity to begin a unit. Cheryl has set this up so that students who finish later won't feel bad because someone else shouted out, "Oh! I get it!" long before others have even begun to look.

Together, the class next discusses why some of the documents were chosen for the silent mystery walk. The students stand, approach a document of their choice, and then explain why this item was important. This is a way that students can move about the room, make choices, and have their voices be heard.

KWL "T" CHART

Cheryl then calls on a student at random to lead the "What you know, what you want to know, what you learned" (KWL "T" chart) activity. Most students love being in charge. Even if they don't, it still gives them the chance to hone their tools for public speaking, something almost everyone has to do at some point in life. When you complete an activity such as this, you won't always want to call on students who will have the right answer. It's important to call on all students over time to give them a chance to be heard.

Some teachers we know use Popsicle sticks in a cup, each with a student's name on it. They draw a stick from the cup, read the name, and then that student responds. We have also used back channels on devices to pose questions and get responses from everyone. Back channeling is the feedback that a listener gives to a speaker to show that he or she is following or understands what the speaker is saying. This invites students into conversation without having to speak out loud. There are a variety of back channels that you can use, but sadly, one of our favorites, TodaysMeet, just closed down. However, there are others that have great value, such as Backchannel Chat (Higgin et al. 2018).

During an activity, we believe that all students can assume responsibility for moving the lesson forward. Students can call on their peers and have them place what they know, for example, about irony on a flip chart in a column labeled "know." The teacher then can ask the class what they would like to know about irony. By asking them to list their questions on a sticky note to be placed on the chart in the "want to know" column later in the activity, all students get to comment on what they are interested in learning about irony—for their own writing as well as within the books they read.

In the next phase of the activity, a student facilitator calls on students to read their sticky note, and then they place the note on the chart. If students don't want to read their note, they can have the student facilitator read it aloud. After several (eight or more) statements have been listed, ask the students to number off into groups. The teacher calls out a number from each group to come to the chart and choose a fact from the "know" and "want to know" area of the KWL "T" chart for their group to research.

Students conduct research on their device of choice (DOC) and discuss the information they have found. Their focus is on their fact of irony, with their (expert) group. Then the groups share out, after the teacher calls on another number and those students share aloud, one at a time from each group.

This chart is saved, and students will write what they have learned on the large chart in the "learned" section of the KWL "T" chart (Lu 2014). The teacher then shares a mentor text, brochure, YouTube, or other documents with the class to give additional examples and details of irony. Any additional information is added to the chart in whichever category is necessary.

The teacher then has the students list the types of irony. They should have examples and a definition in their notes. Even though the teacher directs this activity, there are many pockets of time for the students to individualize the lesson by noting examples of irony in their own reading as well as writing.

There are also opportunities using tech applications such as Padlet and others to support class brainstorming that gives everyone an opportunity to participate (Renard 2017). It's always helpful to check in with your tech support before bringing a new tool into the classroom to be sure the app is not going to require use of students' private data unless the district has endorsed the product for use.

LESSON EVALUATION

Let's review all that students were able to accomplish and all that the teacher did. Students moved around the room quietly, reading, looking, and observing, resembling a detective. The teacher had previously made the KWL "T" chart. (This only has to be done once. The students can create the chart the next time.) Students had a choice of group, choice of what to write on the sticky note, choice of where to research information, choice of which device to use, and choice of seating.

Did the teacher lose any control of the class while the students were exercising these choices? Students will sometimes get off task or misbehave regardless of teacher control. During class activities, we make it a point to walk around and monitor device use to see what students are researching. The teacher might choose to sit next to a student and hear what they are discussing or look at their sticky notes to see what they are writing. All of these actions are being proactive instead of reactive.

Offer sincere praise so your students can hear the good work going on in the room. Comments such as, "It is great that you are looking on appropriate sites for information and that each of you are researching information on irony of your choice" help keep students motivated and their work positive in an activity.

In the irony activity, students were able to move freely as they placed their fact onto the chart. This aspect helped build ownership in the topic and sustained attention. Students were physically moving, recording, analyzing, researching, conversing, cooperating, collaborating, making connections, acquiring new knowledge, and feeling empowered with the knowledge that they acquired. The teacher, prior to the lesson, found several documents of examples of irony, printed them, stuck them to colorful paper and posted them around the room, and researched a variety of examples of irony through YouTube, text, and photos.

After completing the twenty-minute research and sharing activity, the students moved forward to the evaluation part of the lesson. Students watched YouTube clips and viewed the texts and photos in Google Docs before completing an exit slip quick check for understanding. The exit slip asked students to record the definition and list three examples of irony. The students submitted the exit slips to the teacher before starting the next activity. This important component of the lesson plan allows you to evaluate students' knowledge of their own lesson. Exit slips are relatively simple to construct and often address the following:

- Explicit understanding of a key concept, information, or skill
- What questions the student has or what the student does not understand

THE FLOW OF THE CLASS, STUDENTS, AND TEACHER

Students will shift to a different activity about every twenty minutes on the typical day in class. We find this is about enough time to keep students on task before they begin to fidget or lose interest. You can use your phone as a timer so that students are not overly focused on the time. Some students will also set their watch or phone as a timer as well. We see this as a sign of investment.

The Learning Space and Student Autonomy in the Classroom 119

We like to set up students to be in charge of several activities in the room. For example, we may say to a table of students, "The class supply area isn't working out as well as anticipated. Would you please arrange that area and make it work more efficiently for all of us, please?" Students love this opportunity. It is *their* room because we encourage them to make it *theirs*. Also, another group of students might generate a better way to display student work in the class and/or hallway.

We love when students want to take charge of the room. In this case, Michael may give his students enough time to arrange or rearrange the items on the display board and may hint they should add a title that will encourage others to look at their work. We see ownership for the class environments as leading to agency, whether it is bulletin boards, the class library, stations in the room, or even help desk support for other students who are having technology problems. Of course, we, and you, could complete all of these tasks, but why take the fun out of it for the students?

Ensuring that each student in a group participates in deciding who does which part of an activity or project task creates ownership within the group for the work. We always linger around to ensure no one is left out and to monitor how the team works together. We also want to be sure that decisions in groups are equitable and fair and that the work students do is empowering and consistent with the school's vision.

Teachers need their own time to reflect and use metacognition, and this is important to the learning processes you are facilitating. You need time to consider what questions are necessary to ensure all students are engaged and

growing as learners. Did the students complete what you expected of them that day? Did they learn the objective, learning target, or big question? While others were researching something or finishing another task, did some students take on the role of leaders of the class by assisting with what needed to be accomplished for their classroom? How did your classroom environment foster relationships between the students and you?

When students begin to take charge of their own learning and even leading and supporting each other, your role as a teacher changes. You are still in the room to coach, guide, direct, and counsel as needed. However, when students take charge of their learning, they are empowered and thus, feel important, needed, cared for, respected, and trusted within their own classroom. When we shift our power to students, it elevates their autonomy and their choices. The teacher becomes the "guide on the side," as Cheryl says.

Writers' workshop is one area where flow is essential (Stockman 2018). Setting up students to see themselves as writers can be challenging. However, when students see themselves as writers with a story to tell, even the most reluctant writers will begin to record or write their words. Michael has found that most elementary students love to share their writing with at least their friends within the classroom. However, by the time students are in middle school, Cheryl has found that she has to work intensively to get some stu-

dents to write. She often uses strategies that connect students to each other's writing.

Getting to a place where you can have students work in pairs and choose their own partner takes time, but it is also important to express the importance of everyone having a partner. Over time, students learn that if Cheryl has said to organize into partner groups, and a person is left out, another group will just invite that student to their group.

We also have learned the importance of moving around the room and creating some eye contact when students get into groups. No student should be left alone. It is especially important that classmates are not cruel to any students. Teachers have to be on their toes for this not to happen. If it does occur, quickly, but gently, you will need to talk with the students and ask if they were ever alone and without a group. How did that make them feel? Teaching and modeling empathy is crucial in a space for risk. The goal for students is that they jump in and invite that student to join them.

If you know that you are going to conduct an activity where students choose their groups, you could approach quiet or shy students prior to starting the activity and share what the class is about to do. Also, share that they need to go straight to the person they want as their partner. This takes some time for some students. Each student is unique and moves differently for various reasons. As a teacher (and student) in the room, you have to respect that.

EXPERIENCES IN THE CLASSROOM

When it comes to reading, there is a lot of research to support giving students choices of books to read, whether it's Nancie Atwell's work on reading workshop (Atwell and Merkel 2016) or Kelly Gallagher's (Gallagher 2009) research on why students stop reading. Whenever possible, help students find books they find interesting, which may be very different than what you find intriguing. You also may want to set up choices of books that students want to read in small groups as part of a book club or a more formal literature circle strategy.

Finally, sometimes, you may want to allow students to choose from fiction and nonfiction books or posts on a topic they are studying. Occasionally, you will likely want the class to have an experience reading a book together even if no one reads the complete book. All of these represent different choice approaches to reading, whether in elementary, middle, or high school English/language arts.

The trickiest reading unit is when you want everyone to experience a book together. Cheryl does this occasionally, except students organize into groups and each group chooses which chapter they'd like to teach to the class. In one recent unit, students suggested that the class think of how each liked to learn and how some of their favorite teachers taught them their favorite lessons throughout the years. As an activity, students wrote up their plan of how they were going to teach the topic, what materials were needed, and the process for engaging peers. One student said it was as if you were a baker teaching someone how to bake a cake.

The next day, Cheryl demonstrated her chapter as a model. She had each group embark on becoming an expert group on one topic from her chapter, and each group had a task to accomplish. Each group had to decide how they would accomplish the task. After completion of her presentation, members of the class knew that when it was their turn to respond to peer expert groups, they would have to, just as their teacher had done, demonstrate knowledge of their topic, accomplish a task that the chapter expert group had assigned, and also share constructive criticism aloud—a way to help the expert groups, but also their own team, on presentations in the future.

The class brainstormed on a large sheet of paper; then each group began planning. They knew to speak quietly so that the other groups would not hear their ideas. The teacher created a rubric for herself and taught the students how to create one. Each group had their own rubric on what it meant to accomplish the presentation of their chapter, share out, and assess information. The teacher said their rubric could look similar but not the same as her model. The class was focused on each person having a speaking part, a task to complete, and cooperating while they collaborate.

Students took off from there and created their rubric and lesson, and they were ready on presentation day. The teacher asked who should go first. They said that it made sense to go in order of the chapters of the table of contents. Cheryl and Michael know that even giving the students the chance to make simple decisions like this will lead to more autonomy and investment among students.

Some students listed the steps, had the class take notes, and quizzed them at the end. Some had each member of the class engaged as they proceeded through each step. One group split up the class into groups, and each member joined a group and taught them individually. It was an awesome lesson. The students felt like teachers in an authentic setting. It was also powerful for them to see what it takes to plan, problem solve, and prioritize information.

Some students did not talk out of turn as much afterward because they saw what it takes to be in the front of the room. It was also beneficial for them to see what it is like to teach others when they are not paying attention. It was a lesson in tolerance, patience, and collaborative learning. It was an authentic experience with an authentic audience. It is the type of lesson that students will remember fondly well after they have completed their school career.

Cheryl's task was to be a model for how the expert groups maintain attention of other students, create interesting lessons, and share new knowledge. The students in the expert groups also were encouraged to be unique in their presentations, speak loudly and clearly in front of a group, and ensure that members of the class understood the new knowledge. Each student felt empowered, a sense of accomplishment, and a new respect for teachers and those speaking in front of a group. They each learned so much more than the one topic they chose to teach; they learned lifelong lessons.

Where was Cheryl during all of this? She was buzzing around, from group to group, ensuring cooperation and collaboration as well as making sure that knowledge was being shared. Cheryl also monitored the knowledge and techniques being used to ensure that students understood what they were taught.

It was an authentic activity. The teacher had the groups evaluate each of the other groups' work, and the students checked off the rubric, after each person presented their part. They had instant feedback and instant gratification for a job well done.

Could a teacher conduct that activity with every class? Sure! The students and the teacher would tailor it to fit what that class could do successfully and where they might need assistance. Would the teacher do that with every lesson? Probably not, but it could apply to some future lessons.

Students have great ideas. Listen to them. Let them share. Let them be in charge of their learning. They will feel empowered, and it will mean so much more to them if they participate and are engaged. Allow your students to be in front of the class and share their knowledge some of the time.

When students have a common or shared interest and a say in what they are doing, they come through and feel empowered. They want to present to an authentic audience. Allowing them to be in charge of their learning is key. Give them opportunities to make memories, and share their desire to learn with the class as a whole. Give them the keys to knowledge and step back.

WORKS CITED

Atwell, Nancie, and Anne Atwell Merkel. 2016. *The Reading Zone: How to Help Kids Become Passionate, Skilled, Habitual, Critical Readers*. New York: Scholastic Incorporated.

Gallagher, Kelly. 2009. *Readicide: How Schools Are Killing Reading and What You Can Do about It*. Portsmouth, NH: Stenhouse.

Higgin, Tanner, Danny Wagner, Emily Major, Ben Cogswell, George Lopez, and Erin Wilkey Oh. 2018. "3 Backchanneling Websites to Replace TodaysMeet." Common Sense Education. June 12, 2018. https://www.commonsense.org/education/blog/3-backchanneling-websites-to-replace-todaysmeet.

Lu, Jeremy. 2014. "KWL Chart, KWL Chart Template Online." GroupMap—Collaborative Brainstorming and Decision Making. July 18, 2014. https://www.groupmap.com/map-templates/kwl-chart/.

Renard, Lucie. 2017. "8 Intuitive Brainstorm Apps for a Collaborative Classroom." *BookWidgets* (blog). March 3, 2017. https://www.bookwidgets.com/blog/2017/03/8-intuitive-brainstorm-apps-for-a-collaborative-classroom.

Stockman, Angela. 2018. *Hacking the Writing Workshop: Redesign with Making in Mind*. Highland Heights, OH: Times 10.

Chapter Thirteen

A Different Vision of Risk

Differentiation and Individualism in the Classroom

Don't count the days. Make the days count.—Muhammad Ali

QUESTIONS TO PONDER IN THIS CHAPTER

- *What strategies does the teacher use to observe and assess learners to determine their unique needs, capabilities, and cultural frames so that instructional practices can be varied appropriately?*
- *How does the teacher determine what students already know, understand, and can do to inform and plan personalized learning options and daily differentiation instructional strategies?*
- *In what ways does the teacher vary the pace, seating, groups, time, movement, and activities to meet the needs of every student and offer individual choices?*
- *Does the teacher use multiple indicators of progress and assessments for and of learning, rather than traditional grading practices, to share formative feedback and growth information relevant to what each learner has accomplished?*

INDIVIDUALISM AND DIFFERENTIATION

The beginning of the year always engenders an excitement and enthusiasm among almost all students and the teachers who serve them. When students hop off the bus or exit family cars on the first day of school, anyone who observes them entering school begins immediately to see the diversity among young people. Diversity runs so much more deeply than a child's color, native language, or economic background. Some children come to school on that first day with stories ready to share.

Others are quiet observers. They have varied interests. Some come with well-honed "school skills" while others have had little school experience. Background knowledge of the world and the content of curriculum differ as well across students. However, they share on the first day—from our professional experiences—something that is foundational to learning.

We've never seen a learner who begins the school year with the idea that he or she will fail. Instead, we see learners who come to school with an intention to thrive even if their prior experiences have not been successful. However, when a school community employs a one-size-fits-all or standardized approach to learning, rather than seeing each student as an individual, students—particularly those with risk factors—may quickly disengage and disconnect from the learning work.

KID WATCHING AND COMING TO KNOW THE UNIQUENESS OF EACH LEARNER

Students are as different as snowflakes falling from the sky, and even if students share commonalities and connections, they still are individuals who need individual attention. When teachers engage learners in a variety of "how you learn" activities in the beginning of school, it is obvious that each classroom includes learners who vary across a continuum of demographics, learning preferences, experiences, and interests. To personalize learning, every student needs access to resources and instructional strategies tailored so his or her needs are met. This does not happen by chance. As Carol Tomlinson, professor at the University of Virginia and differentiation expert, says:

> One of the first things I look for are teacher-student connections. Does this seem to be a teacher who is really paying attention to the kids, who's going out of his or her way to study them and understand what makes them tick? To be effective with differentiation, a teacher really needs to talk with the kids, ask them their opinions on things, sit down with them for a minute or two to see how things are going, and listen to them and find out what they are interested in. All that feeds back into instruction. And teacher-student connections not only help teachers plan what to do with kids, it also provides motivation for differentiation: If I can see kids as real individual human beings, I'm going to be much more invested in helping them learn and grow individually. (Quoted in Rebora 2008)

Designing a personalized or differentiated classroom is a learning imperative that begins with figuring out the strengths and assets of each learner.

This sets the stage for visualizing each learner as capable of surmounting learning challenges, rising up to achieve, and offering insight and value to the class community. This starts with coming to understand what our learners (or "users") desire for themselves and how they see themselves as learners, their interests, their strengths, and what they hope for.

"How you learn" activities vary based on the age of learners but have one concept in common: teachers can gain insight as well as the learners from their time engaged in reflection and metacognition. For example, teachers might either survey or interview older learners with questions relevant to their learning experiences:

- Tell me about a time when you had fun learning and why it was fun.
- What makes learning challenging for you and why?
- What are you interested in doing outside of school? Inside school?
- If you could stay longer in any class, what would it be and why?
- What advice do you have for me that will help me help you in this class?
- How do you prefer to learn?
- If you could choose to show me what you have learned, how might you do that?

With younger or older learners, you might figure out similar background understanding by setting up centers over a week and allowing students to choose where they want to work. Make notes of how they choose physically to work—standing, seated, or on the floor. Make notes of what kinds of options they choose from the center choices. Who do they work with, or do they appear to work alone? Ask them questions about why they seem to like some choices more than others.

You also can find survey and inventories online or through a school counselor that may help you develop background knowledge of each child (Shumow and Schmidt 2013). But *remember this*: a student once said that teachers always survey them about what they like at the beginning of the year but seldom discuss the results with students or seem to use the information. If you pursue design thinking as a model for developing experiences that meet the needs of users in your classroom, assessing user preferences and feedback is a critical first step—a step that begins with empathy for each learner.

One strategy to ensure you will use information you gain from engaging with learners individually is to keep a record of the needs, interests, and perspectives of each student. This document is designed to highlight each student's learning needs, their strengths, and their interests. Once you record this information, possibly in an easily accessible document online, honoring each child by interacting with them as individuals is a first step at the beginning of the year to building positive regard and relationships with students.

This does not mean you must teach thirty different lessons. However, it does mean planning ahead to alter lessons through a variety of teaching strategies, choice projects, and media designed to engage every student in the learning process.

In particular, approaching your planning and implementation of instruction through a culturally responsive lens supports learners sensing that you value what they bring to the classroom in terms of cultural knowledge, competencies, and language. For example, while there may be a place for everyone reading a novel together for the purpose of seminar discussions, if a learner who has language barriers for any reason is not able to use text-to-speech applications, it limits the learner's access to curriculum and to peer-to-peer learning.

If the reading always selected comes from the traditional canon of literature, whether picture books or authors such as Hemingway, some students will not find themselves in what they read. How do you expand reading choices to include a range of diverse selections? How will you engage your students in active learning that supports them to bring their individual strengths, knowledge, and experiences into the classroom culture so that each is individually validated? As noted author, keynoter, and middle school teacher Pernille Ripp says:

> It is not enough to have diverse books in our classrooms if we are too afraid to discuss diversity and what the lack of humanity for others does to our democracy. It is not enough to say "You matter" and then do nothing to change the world that we live in. Or to celebrate diversity and then not accept a child for who they truly are, differences and all. It is not enough to say we are an ally if our actions don't match our words. I don't need 100 clones of me, I need to create more opportunities for the students to do the hard work. To offer them an opportunity to decide. To create an environment where they can discover their own opinion. Where they can explore the world, even when it is ugly so that they can decide which side of history they want to fall on. (Ripp 2017)

SUCCESS IN THE CLASSROOM: SHIFTING CONTROL TO THE STUDENT

It is rewarding, as a teacher, to see the "aha" moments in a learner that result from changes in instructional practices. Make it a challenge to see an "aha" moment on each child's face. This is a charge we've incorporated into our own classroom work with learners. Students need to master what they both want and are expected to learn. That can be assessed in a variety of ways, but when they present and share their learning through a video documentary they've made or a service project they've completed, their learning mastery becomes authentic and deep, transferable as life (not just school) learning.

Students are fully capable of determining how they want to demonstrate their learning, even with constraints that you may set. Providing the opportunity to make choices in how they learn and how they show what they learned enables young people to feel successful.

Once students accomplish the task at hand, give up your own need to announce that they can move onto the next task. Have it already set up in a way that allows the students to recognize what is expected next. This could be recorded online in a daily agenda such as in Google Classroom or on a visible flip chart or digital board that all can see. This allows the teacher time to work with those who require assistance, and those who are ready to move forward are able to do so on their own accord.

This places the responsibility on the students to take charge of their learning. As they finish tasks, they also feel more confident and successful. When students are coached to work in this way on areas of curricular focus coupled with personal interest, classroom management becomes a function of their internal motivation versus external control.

That should be one of the teacher's goals for each student. Teachers should expect success from their students, and building confidence along the way helps that become more of a reality. As students move on to the next task, they are less likely to distract others in class. When they move ahead, they will not be expected to complete tedious assignments all on the same topic. Instead, they might begin writing a story including a concept that was previously taught. They may use online sources to delve deeper into a subject. Students may develop a presentation that demonstrates their understanding of a former, current, or future concept.

When students are able to shift from one task to the next, either individually or in collaborative teams without teacher direction, the entire class becomes part of a differentiated process that does not call attention to students who need additional help or holds back learners who are ready to move forward. The user experience becomes a function of learning embedded in enriching activities, interest-driven projects, small-group or individual attention from the teacher, whole-group instruction as needed, all headed toward outcomes that challenge all learners and instruction that engages young people differently (Tomlinson 2014).

For example, students in a class may be writing a narrative about content they are studying or something in which they are interested, choosing the tool they need to best help them record what they want to write. A student, dependent upon his or her writing skill and regardless of age, may or may not add enough details to the story. You, as the teacher, must both support intervention as well as enrichment needs of each student based upon where students are on the learning continuum.

This means daily work with students individually or in small groups while the rest of the class works independently. When a student who needs additional support begins to grasp a concept or skill, you can step away to circulate around the room, possibly checking stories for clarity, topic, details, and examples to support learners while doing quick individual conferences or writing a personal note to share feedback.

In such a class setting, students are taught based on individual needs with the goal that each learner moves forward as they master competencies. As the teacher circulates, he or she whispers to each group to share their stories (if they so choose) with another student in the class, another class, a parent at home, or even another trusted educator in the school. Google Docs serve as a great collaboration resource in the classroom, allowing collaboration inside and outside of the school environment.

Nothing increases the potential of young people to use their voice in powerful ways than learning to communicate—writing song lyrics or a play, creating a YouTube or Vimeo video, building a social media marketing plan to promote an activist platform, writing a story based on something of interest, or creating an autobiography picture book. These all lead to agency among learners and a belief in their own capability to influence.

Each student will reach the point of writing as a powerful communication tool through a different pathway, but eventually they all arrive. The teacher may assign the topic for writing or allow students to choose, with the goal of demonstrating how they can utilize the concept that was taught. Some students will write even in the evening, sharing their story with others, allowing others to join in and write as well.

Again, writing in Google Docs allows this collaboration to be possible. As we say to learners, "The more writers, the merrier." As the students write and collaborate, their confidence grows. More confidence leads to a higher success rate, a sense of personal efficacy, and internalized motivation to pursue learning with a passion.

When students see other students' work in the content they are learning, they see that youth voices matter. With teacher facilitation, they begin to share with whom they choose to share, and they feel safe doing so. They tend to accept peer feedback with more confidence when they can choose peer feedback partners than if forced to work with a partner selected by the teacher.

However, the role of the teacher continues to be important in the learning process as the teacher reads individual writing as well and adds his or her feedback, ideas, suggestions, and questions, sometimes in face-to-face miniconferences and sometimes in Google Docs. We have learned from colleagues and in our own work that age is not a limiter for using Google Docs or other online resources to capture a student's writing, particularly students who are reluctant writers who can be advantaged through use of universal design for learning apps such as speech-to-text (Krakower and Plante 2015).

We've seen students using back channels such as TodaysMeet or dictation apps embedded in software to put their ideas and words on the page. This helps children who are in the first stages of transferring oral speech to written speech, whether English-language learners, students with disabilities, or young students who simply are learning to match the auditory sounds of words with written language.

New technologies such as Flipgrid or SeeSaw offer ways to bridge home to school connectivity when students are supported to post screenshots of their written work and even video of themselves explaining what they are doing or in a miniconference with a teacher.

We have learned that shifting power to students from us increases their engagement in learning, allows them to take control of their own work, and creates a context for learning in which they are partners with peers and us. The use of technologies that empower learners to work interdependently and independently actually frees us to be facilitators and guides of the personalization process in the classroom.

We also have increased our own on-task learning time because we spend less time addressing off-task behaviors or redirecting students. We have become more joyful educators as we have learned to give up command and control strategies and replace those with strategies that empower personal learning efficacy among the students we teach.

DESIGNING LESSONS FOR LEARNING: A FOCUS ON OUTCOMES AND ENGAGING LEARNERS IN THE ASSESSMENT EXPERIENCE

The students in the classroom are learning the same curriculum, at a different pace, and participating in different grouping and collaboration patterns while making choices as they proceed. They are learning at their own pace and along their own paths of learning. We have learned the importance of recording what we notice and to record that in student learning profiles, online, or in a journal.

We have found from "kid watching" interactions and observations regarding academic progress, learning preferences, social emotional dimensions of learning, and other critical knowledge of each student that we become more tuned in to learners as individuals and that it helps us ask questions, reinforce interests, and make sense of next steps to scaffold. In addition, these private entries include information pertinent to some students' accommodation needs as specified in 504 and IEP plans. Creating student profiles sets the stage for teachers to reflect on the needs of individual students as they design learning plans.

In more personalized classrooms, teachers are knowledgeable of individuals, and students with diverse capabilities, learning preferences, and academic achievement levels succeed and grow together. Most teachers record information in a manner that best suits them. We consider it imperative that the teacher knows the unique needs of students. Every lesson should be constructed to help every student find success somewhere along the way. In fact, student diversity becomes a strength, supporting learners to learn with and from each other.

Such classrooms become culturally responsive, differentiated, and authentic spaces of high expectations. The lessons over the course of a unit meet a goal that parents, students, teachers, administration, and the community can share and support as one—that *all* children develop the competencies they need to be successful in school and life. Such success is possible, and we know from our own experiences this can be accomplished.

What is the key to effective design of lessons for learning? First, teachers need to focus on varying instructional strategies. Teachers may use a novel, an informational text, a YouTube clip, or another source so that students can access the same information based on their preferences and interest in a particular media. As teachers plan with the end in mind of personalization, they design lessons that are purposefully flexible and naturally lead to student differentiation.

Such lessons engage students and benefit students rather than simply keep students "busy." When you look around our classrooms, you will only occasionally see students all working on the same task or in direct instruction. Our goals are the same for our learners, but the activities, interactions with peers and with us, and the outputs from students vary greatly on any given day.

Because of how we design lessons, you might see some students working collaboratively in a small group, others reading, and some working on devices to access information, do research, or create project work. Formative assessment is ongoing and may include some decontextualized items as well as performance tasks or simply our observations.

We begin lesson design by asking the simple question, How will each student best learn the concept? This should always be the initial thought as a lesson is being developed. If a teacher has access to using an instructional technologist or teacher coach within the building, we have found collaboration with the specialist to be of great value in the planning process. If not, consider how you might network with virtual peers in social media such as Twitter to seek resources and suggestions for activities.

You can find experts everywhere who help you make your lessons "pop!" We are often reminded when we work together and with our own team members that regardless of a teacher's level of experience and success, we can all make changes that improve our design of lessons, even after thirty-five years of teaching!

Consider how you can use the newest technology you have available to open up new paths to learning in your lessons. Students relish the chance to try out different ways to develop their own learning and will "chomp" at the work when they have a choice among potential learning opportunities available to them.

Remember, our job is to ensure that our students learn as we teach, not just to cover a curriculum. What do students need to excel in class? Are their needs being met? Is the teacher modeling what it means to continue to be a lifelong learner? How might you plan to include activities and strategies to address the needs of special education students, students with deep academic strengths, English-learning students, and of course all of the students?

It is a great feeling to complete the front-loading of a lesson and everything you wanted to accomplish falls into place. Students, regardless of academic level, are learning and demonstrating knowledge of the concepts being taught. Nothing is more important to the success of a lesson for learning design than knowing each student's strengths, needs, interests, and learning preferences. This allows you to evolve lessons through each conversation you have with a learner. Students love this individual attention, and when they get to be the center of the conversation with you, they can give you useful feedback that matters as well.

As you are designing lessons, consider the numerous media that a student can use to demonstrate knowledge of the concept to be learned. These media should be varied, and the students should have some choices for their use in an assignment.

Before a child begins and definitely before any student reaches the time for a final presentation of his or her learning, whether in a performance assessment task or a project, you should also design into a lesson how you will model a rubric, how exemplars will be shared, and even how you will model a presentation and provide time for students to ask questions and comment on the teacher's presentation. When you model what success looks like and leave space for that within the lesson for the learning plan, it also gives you a chance to encourage students to add their creativity and unique interests into the task or project. This does not happen by chance.

One strategy we have included as an activity in our lesson design provides time for students to learn how to create a rubric that they follow in sharing what they have learned with you and peers. There are hundreds of ways students can show what they know and understand. Let the students work on how they want to show you and coach them on what quality work will look like to you and to them. Give them the time and space to do this without feeling pressure from you.

If they do choose to present, prior to the presentation ensure that students have a chance to explain their rubric to the class. Create an activity in your lesson design to engage the class in learning how to listen to a presentation, and how they will give feedback upon completion of an oral presentation both in asking questions and analyzing the project.

You also may build in time in your lesson design for students to practice their presentation with another student during class to improve elocution. We have found that the process of student creating their own rubric, the learning process, selection of a final product(s), and how they plan to engage an audience allows students numerous choices that can lead to success.

This helps students to learn to make simple choices and then analyze the results. Even if their project was not a complete success, these planned experiences allow students to develop competencies essential to success in life. Sometimes learning failures are more important than learning successes.

Failing . . . failing is a part of life. After all, who has a life that is smooth sailing constantly without any strife? Experiencing what failure looks and feels like and how to rise above it while they are in school with the support of the class and teacher is critical for young people so that they have a chance to make sense of failure in the context of learning rather than waiting until they are on their own in adult life when failure may have greater consequences.

When students don't successfully complete a task, it provides an opportunity to consider that as a learning experience. Will they blame others? Improve? Redo the task? Give up? It is up to us, as teachers, to be present, encourage, and support positive reinforcement of how to handle failures as well as successes. However, grades should not be used to punish students for failing to learn.

While that may challenge the thinking of some, we operate from a mastery model where our goal for students keeps them in a cycle in which they fix their work to meet expected outcomes and goals. No student, in our opinion, should reach the point of summative assessment without the skills and knowledge to meet criteria for success. This happens when students' formative assessments are used to scaffold them to success.

CLASSROOM ENVIRONMENT AND CLIMATE: CREATING INCLUSIVE LEARNING COMMUNITIES

Developing a positive climate in a class is crucial and begins with work to create an environment in which differentiated learning opportunities lead to a norm of student success. A teacher cannot expect students to take a risk and fail if they do not feel confident and safe in the classroom.

In classrooms where learning is personalized through differentiation, students feel safe and develop confidence. Providing learners with choices helps them begin to feel a sense of learning control, and success in their work leads to a belief in their own agency. Linking how we create a culture of positive learning to our design of lessons for learning is critical to the process of building inclusive learning communities, staging your classroom to enable learners to be successful.

It is smart to have a variety of craft materials in the room labeled "craft closet" or "craft cabinet." Students should have access to this cabinet without asking to complete projects. How does a teacher gain numerous materials for this space? A teacher asks parents for donations of materials at Back-to-School Night, or even during the student/parent orientation. Create a list and disseminate to parents, listing what their child and classmates may need during the year. For example, a teacher might ask for large and small baggies, construction paper, newspapers, cardstock paper, leftover wallpaper, wallpaper borders, marbles, flour, buttons, material, gravel/rocks with color, hard and soft clay, paints, paintbrushes of all sizes, small pieces of craft wood, yarn, string, fishing string, et cetera. Parents will donate, so have the craft closet ready!

Differentiation is similar to scaffolding and is important to move students along from where they are to where they need to be in the learning continuum. In differentiation, the teacher may give some students a different passage or text to read, which is more on their level, but still covers the same concept, or give the entire class the choice to choose the type of text which explains it best to them.

Scaffolding is "chunking" the material so that students feel successful in both learning and demonstrating knowledge of the concept learned. Many teachers run the two simultaneously, where it may be difficult to see the differences; but the needs are met for each child, which is the goal.

Differentiation sounds like it may take a lot of work on the teacher's part, but really it is what needs to be done to know the students and their strengths, areas that need improvement, and interests. Gone are the days where the teacher stands in front of the room for the entire class and lectures. Traditional teaching is out the door, and making connections and relationships with the students is innovative.

If you choose to lecture, then lecture using technology, manipulatives, photos, charts, and guest speakers. Work toward not lecturing for the duration of the class. Each student can sustain attention for a short period of time. The block of time teaching should be divided into the number of minutes for that age group. Middle school scholars can usually sustain a fifteen- to twenty-minute talk, and that should include engagement. The teacher should then adjust the lesson so that the students are more active with movement and out of their seats. A teacher needs to differentiate per student per class. Know your students and their needs, and this can be accomplished.

Students move on to exemplifying knowledge of the concept taught as each is ready. Presentation can occur with elbow partners, small-group members, the entire class, the entire grade level, or in the evening as a "coffeehouse." Presenting to an authentic audience is key. This makes learning the entire concept worthwhile for the students. It is also building a climate of acceptance and one that fosters positive relationships.

Parents, relatives, neighbors, child caretakers, and others love to hear the students present. This makes the lesson real for the students. It is not difficult to plan, have your students plan the "social gathering." All of these experiences assist the students in learning how to learn, apply lifelong techniques and skills needed for the workplace and in life in general.

The idea of differentiation is to preassess and see where students are academically, teach them, and move them forward. Each student is taught where he or she is and then moved forward through rich, varied experiences for growth and achievement. It is like what a doctor, an attorney, a day care provider will do. Preassess, see where an individual is currently, vary the approach to meet the needs of the individual, and have some type of postassessment to determine growth and improvement. Everyone is constantly learning.

LIFELONG LEARNING

Teachers need to demonstrate to students that learning continues for life. Show students that you have a book in your purse or school bag for when your tires are being changed or you are waiting for a doctor's appointment. Modeling is key and can be a profound example for students. Another great idea is to discuss the books that the teacher has read with his or her students. That demonstrates for students that teachers continue to read and write.

A teacher could also share a rough draft of a chapter in a book to show the students the work they are completing. For example, in other disciplines, a math teacher can place a checkbook under the document camera to model how a checkbook is balanced. A history teacher can write, again using the document camera, a critique of a new historical nonfiction book. These are examples teachers could demonstrate for students. All of these examples would help students see that reading, writing, and learning are lifelong endeavors.

Students mimic behavior. When conflicts arise, teachers should model using resources as a means to fix the problem. For example, if a teacher struggles to make straight lines, then utilize a ruler. That simple task will help students make similar decisions on their own. Talk your way through the situation, aloud. If a teacher asks students to write about their life experiences, the teacher can exemplify, either on the board, or on the document camera, his or her thought process while writing. Reading and writing is accomplished through all curricula.

When a student asks a question in which the teacher is unsure of the answer, the teacher can say, "Oh! I'm not sure about that. I need to research it." Then, take the time to demonstrate this research process to students, and continue writing. Allow students to hear and observe how the teacher thinks as a writer, as a mathematician, or as an artist. The risk of saying "I don't know" is empowering. It shows vulnerability but also growth as a learner.

WORKS CITED

Krakower, Billy, and Sharon Lepage Plante. 2015. *Using Technology to Engage Students with Learning Disabilities*. Thousand Oaks, CA: Corwin.

Rebora, Anthony. 2008. "Making a Difference." *Education Week Teacher* 2, no. 1 (September). https://www.edweek.org/tsb/articles/2008/09/10/01tomlinson.h02.html.

Ripp, Pernille. 2017. "On Hard Conversations and Having Courage." *Pernille Ripp* (blog). July 20, 2017. https://pernillesripp.com/2017/07/20/on-hard-conversations-and-having-courage/.

Shumow, Lee, and Jennifer A. Schmidt. 2013. "Student Interest Inventory." Northern Illinois University E-Teams. 2013.https://www.niu.edu/eteams/pdf_s/VALUE_ StudentInterestInventory.pdf.

Tomlinson, Carol Ann. 2014. *The Differentiated Classroom: Responding to the Needs of All Learners*. 2nd ed. Alexandria, VA: ASCD.

Chapter Fourteen

Elementary School Learning Spaces

Do not train children to learning by force and harshness, but direct them to it by what amuses their minds, so that you may be better able to discover with accuracy the peculiar bent of the genius of each.—Plato

QUESTIONS TO PONDER IN THIS CHAPTER

- *How can a traditional elementary learning space become a space for risk?*
- *What are some instructional strategies that work in a space for risk in an elementary setting?*
- *What role should an elementary student play in a space for risk?*
- *What role should an elementary teacher play in a space for risk?*

THE ELEMENTARY CLASSROOM

Two children are crouched over what appears to be a drone to adult observers. The murmur of the children's voices morphs into conversation as adults who are visiting the class move closer. The students are getting ready to test-fly the class's drone. The teacher moves over and says, "Why don't you take that outside—maybe Tishia [another student] can go with you since she's been teaching others how to fly it and capture videos."

Around the class, some students are curled up on beanbags reading books. A few students on their 1:1 devices are building an early colonial settlement in Minecraft. One student is on an exercise bike and appears to be listening to a mobile device. The teacher says that this child is listening to an audiobook, and the activity of the bike helps him sustain attention as he listens. Six students are gathered around a large, standing touchscreen, drawing solutions to a math problem.

No matter where one looks, this class is engaged, working intently and intentionally, and it's hard to tell where the teacher is. In fact, during the entire observation, the teacher's voice is never raised above that of the class. The low profile of the teacher during this portion of class doesn't mean that one wouldn't see students all gathered together later in the morning for a short minilesson directed by the teacher to introduce some new ways to edit their writing for punctuation errors.

The visitors take away several thoughts from the site visit based on their observations and interaction with elementary students and teachers. Space matters. Tools matter. The teacher's expertise matters the most. They have observed what a well-orchestrated, flexible learning space looks like—and how the teacher also supports learning spontaneity within that environment. They have seen students working on the same competency outcomes that are embedded in the district's High School 2022 profile of the graduate: critical thinking, collaborative teamwork, creative production, knowledge acquisition, and citizenship ("High School 2022," n.d.).

They realize that this is a class that has more than 50 percent economically disadvantaged students. Yet it's hard to tell which students receive special education, English-language learning, or gifted services. This is by design

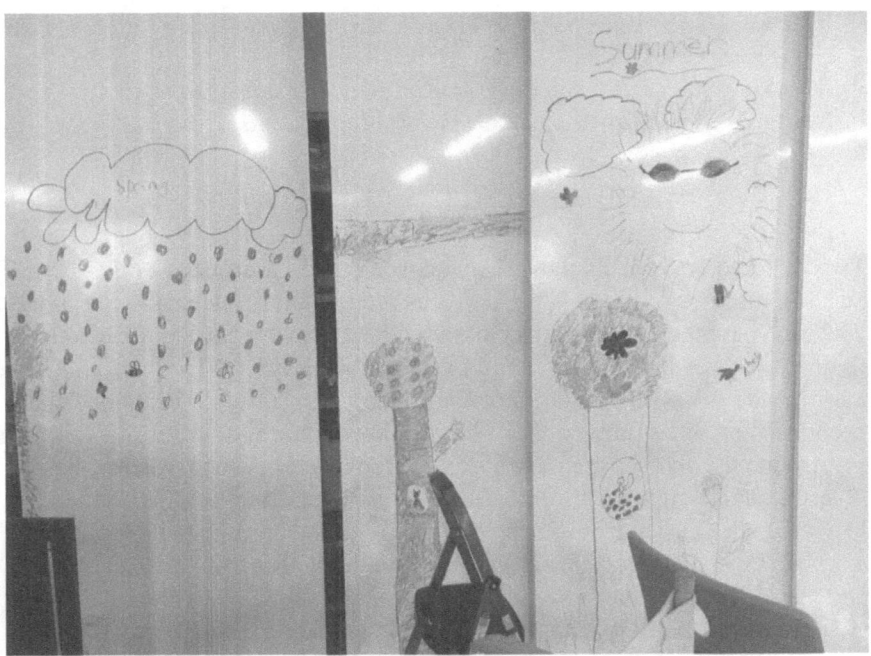

and shows a school community that has embraced diversity through a culturally responsive lens.

The elementary learning space is similar and dissimilar to the middle and high school classroom. Elementary students are interested and invested in topics that many middle and high school students would find childish. Even so, the energy and engagement that is often seen in an elementary classroom should be desired in middle and high school settings.

In turn, the commitment that middle and high school students demonstrate in completing their work is desired in the elementary setting. All three academic settings can work well when there is a thoughtful instructional plan in place that challenges students to embrace failure while building endurance for learning in a positive environment.

Elementary students need time to explore, play, socialize, and collaborate (DeRuy 2016). These four instructional elements should be the basis for most of the lessons developed. In addition to these four instructional elements, time must be considered when planning lessons. Elementary school schedules can and often do hinder creative learning time. This must be changed. The pressure of time should not weigh on the shoulders of elementary students.

Not all students are the same. Their abilities, likes, and dislikes are different. Teachers often develop great learning experiences for students, but a lack of sufficient time eliminates students from experiencing the full potential of the lesson. In order for exploration, play, socialization, and collaboration to contribute to a space for risk, time and schedules must be amended to allow students an appropriate amount of time to learn on their level. The schedule should be flexible, such as if a class needs additional time to complete science experiments.

EXPLORATION, PLAY, SOCIALIZATION, AND COLLABORATION IN A SPACE FOR RISK

Exploring is a necessary aspect of a space for risk. Students need to be able to explore units of study instead of being told explicitly what they are expected to know. Learning is not the retainment of information. It is a messy process that relies on individuals having the time and opportunity to learn in the way that best suits them. Constant direct instruction and limiting student-driven academic decisions will pull learners away from the curriculum. They should be given ample time to explore and connect on their level. This will enable the students to develop a connection with the standards.

The curriculum is a mandatory part of public education. Even so, it doesn't have to be an enemy in the classroom. Let the curriculum be a door to other topics. Develop instructional strategies that enable students to explore the information so they feel connected with the curriculum. Allow them to investigate and decide what they find important before bombarding them with standards. This simple strategy will help students build an authentic relationship with the information. Instead of it being forced upon them, now the students will yearn to learn more because their interest has been piqued.

Activities like the one described above take time. A typical lesson plan usually begins with a hook to capture students' interest. This initial exploration might take multiple classes. That is okay. The time spent will be well worth it when the students are more invested in the product. The students will be ready to move on at different times, and it's important the schedule allows that flexibility.

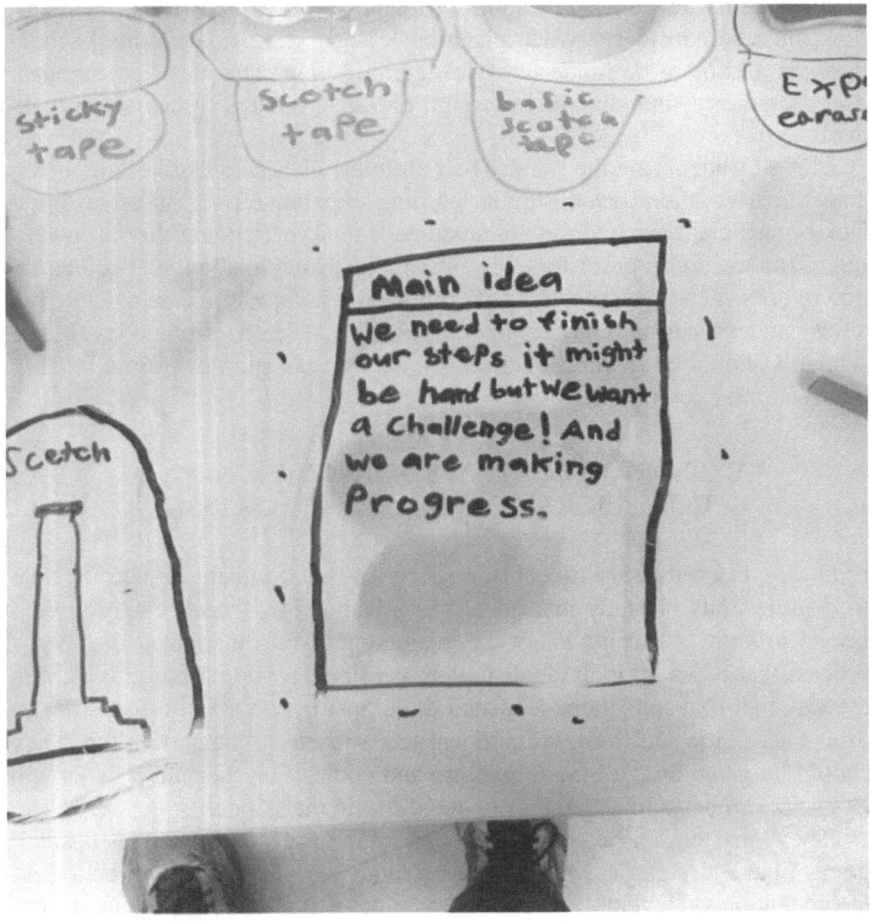

After students have explored the topic on their own, teachers can begin to refocus the students on the standards. During exploration, some students would have already learned and studied some of the information listed in the standards or learned how to use tools that others want to learn to use as well. Teachers should engage these students in the teaching process ("Tech Buddies: Building Technology Skills through Peer Teaching" 2017).

Give them the chance to teach the class on what they discovered. Their exploration becomes a great learning experience for all when it is shared with the entire class. Moreover, their energy and excitement will help build a similar feeling throughout the classroom. This shows the students that their voice and their learning is important to the teacher.

After introducing the standards, the students can begin to play. Play is a tremendously important part of the learning process. Regardless of instructional level, play can become the basis for most lesson plans. Learners need time to experiment before being expected to demonstrate their understanding. Instructional lessons that allow time for play will see better overall student performance.

Elementary classrooms need to have tangible objects in place for the students. It should be an emporium of learning, which relies on teachers setting up a learning space that caters to many different learning styles and interests. Elementary teachers should do as much as they can to set up the classroom, but they also must leave space for student input and decisions. The students should be allowed to voice their opinion about the space and the resources available in the space.

The curricular standards should be shared directly with the students. Inform them so that they are clear on the learning objectives. From there, the ball can be handed off to the students. Teachers should facilitate the learning process by offering advice and direction, but the teacher should not dictate every student decision. The students need this freedom to invest in the curriculum.

If there are students who need more instruction, the teacher can pull them aside in small groups to work directly with them. Direct instruction can have a powerful impact in the classroom when it is not overused or used as the sole strategy to help struggling students. Furthermore, direct instruction in a small-group setting is often more beneficial than direct instruction with the entire class.

Even so, it should not always be the immediate answer for those students who are challenged with the curriculum. Too often academic interventions lead to students sitting more and working in an overly structured environment that limits their decision-making, creativity, and collaboration. Beyond exploration and play, socialization and collaboration are key elements in a space for risk. For the most part, students are naturally social. They want to talk and share. Teachers should take advantage of this common characteristic and use it as an instructional tool in the classroom.

Collaboration in the classroom will often lead to more creativity and critical thinking. It is also an important lifelong skill that elementary students will use as they progress through their academic and professional career. Problem solving is another common by-product of socialization and collaboration. In learning to work with each other, students begin to see themselves as capable of teaching and even giving feedback to another student, reinforcing the idea that students are capable of working as a team to learn together ("I Noticed & I Wondered" 2015).

Teachers are not in the classroom to resolve every problem. The students need to build their empathy for each other by working through problems in the classroom. Whether those problems are academic or social, students need to understand the power of communication and compromise.

Discovering a solution for a problem can be very empowering for students and will give them more confidence in the classroom. Furthermore, there is potential for less learning when teachers are consistently solving the majority of classroom problems for the students. Students who are struggling with a concept often just need more time to explore and play rather than an answer from the instructor.

Exploration, play, socialization, and collaboration are four key components to a space for risk in an elementary classroom. When these four ingredients are mixed with a student-driven, project-based, and/or problem-based instructional plan, the students will build confidence in their academic ability, feel safer in the learning space, and be more inclined to take more risks in the classroom.

THE TEACHER-STUDENT RELATIONSHIP IN THE ELEMENTARY CLASSROOM

Elementary students are naturally inquisitive. They seek answers. Schools need to tap into their inquisitiveness and use it as tool for engagement. If the curriculum is forced on the students with little to no input from them, their desire to learn new information will lessen. Conversely, if the space urges students to explore and gives them ample opportunities to be involved in the learning process, their interest in the curriculum will increase.

When working in the classroom, elementary students need movement. They should not be expected to sit for long periods of time without it. Ideally, the space would enable student choice when it comes to movement. As discussed previously, giving students the power to make instructional decisions in the classroom is essential.

Those instructional decisions will include the freedom to complete work in a position of comfort. For many kids, comfort will include moving around the room without fear that their movement will lead to disciplinary action. As they work, let them base their seating on the task at hand.

Elementary students especially need positive reinforcement and a positive learning environment. Relationship building is very crucial with all students, but this is very true with elementary students. Young learners want to feel a connection with their teacher. Educators should strive to connect with every student in the classroom. Making a positive impact on each student will also help with academic confidence.

A positive learning environment will ease student stress while also teaching them about empathy. Teachers should understand their students well enough to appreciate them for who they are as individuals. Their compassion and understanding will help build a classroom environment that pushes students to think and feel the same way. Teachers should model empathy so that students understand how and when to show it. A classroom filled with empathetic teachers and students will also be a classroom that is open to mistakes and failures.

Academic choice is another important element of the elementary classroom. Giving elementary students academic choice will build engagement while also helping them discover new passions. Not everything learned in the classroom has to be curriculum based. Students need opportunities to just be learners without the curriculum shaping their learning decisions.

Granted, time, or lack thereof, makes this challenging in the standard-based era of education, but it is possible. There are many ways to tie standards to student-driven learning as long as the teacher is committed to doing so. It might take more work and effort, but the students deserve the opportunity.

A space for risk in the elementary setting is paramount. If students are not given the chance to risk in elementary school, how will they know how to do it in life? If young learners are scared to make mistakes early on, that fear will increase as they get older. During their elementary years, teachers should promote mistakes as great learning opportunities.

This will lead to students understanding the value of failure. In the end, that mind-set will help foster more creativity in students while also challenging them to pursue their passions in life.

WORKS CITED

DeRuy, Emily. 2016. "Students Who Play Well Do Better in School." *Atlantic*, September 13, 2016. https://www.theatlantic.com/education/archive/2016/09/learning-through-play/499703/.

"High School 2022." n.d. Albemarle County Public Schools. Accessed July 8, 2018. https://www2.k12albemarle.org/acps/division/hs2022/Pages/Overview.aspx.

"I Noticed & I Wondered." 2015. The Teaching Channel video, 3:01. https://www.teachingchannel.org/videos/student-to-student-feedback-nea.

"Tech Buddies: Building Technology Skills through Peer Teaching." 2017. Edutopia. May 3, 2017. https://www.edutopia.org/video/tech-buddies-building-technology-skills-through-peer-teaching.

Chapter Fifteen

Middle School Learning Spaces

Let us think of education as the means of developing our greatest abilities, because in each of us there is a private hope and dream which, fulfilled, can be translated into benefit for everyone and greater strength for our nation.
—John F. Kennedy

QUESTIONS TO PONDER IN THIS CHAPTER

- *How often do middle school students move in the classroom?*
- *Are your middle school students making important instructional and comfort choices in the classroom?*
- *Are students aware of the support they have in school?*
- *How important is it to make connections with middle school students?*

A MIDDLE SCHOOL SPACE FOR RISK

What should a learning space look like for a middle school student? To maximize a positive learning atmosphere, the environment must be a safe zone so that learners can approach you with questions, ideas, frustrations, and learning intentions. Middle schools are a transitional space for students who have just left elementary schools and who as adolescents are physically, emotionally, and cognitively changing at a rapid pace.

To accommodate the changes in middle school learners, it is important that classrooms be comfortable environments in which students feel confident in who they are and how they choose to interact—or not—with peers. As you set high expectations for learning through a playlist of challenging options that reflect curricular themes, the menu of activities allows students

with a range of developing competencies to individually and collaboratively complete project work (Socol 2012).

We believe that classrooms should reflect the personality of the class—decorated in bright or soft colors, with curtains, several lamps, quiet background music, and fans that provide not just a breeze but also white noise for students who need that. The room is full of books for students to read, no matter the content of the curriculum. In a math room, there may be books about mathematicians who started out not knowing what they wanted to do as a career.

Now these mathematicians are physicists, business managers of a car dealership, data analysts, nurses, or engineers for NASA. There may also be books about animals, airplanes, planets, or anything else that interests the students. A student should always have access to a book in some format.

This safe zone allows students to inquire about the lesson, discuss current events, or to share something on their mind with the teacher or peers. In the class, there is a low buzzing sound of students collaborating with each other. They may be debriefing a recent assessment with a partner, working in a small group on a project, or meeting individually with the teacher.

Some students may be sharing a project they created with a partner. In this safe zone, students feel free to ask questions without negative responses

from either the students or the teacher. Sharing with each other is a risk that students are willing to make when the atmosphere of the classroom is conducive to feeling trust, extending trust, using a respectful tone with others, and knowing that if you can't do something you will not become the target for hurtful behaviors.

INSTRUCTIONAL IDEAS TO DEVELOP STUDENT AUTONOMY

You can ask a student to lead a class discussion on a topic that the student is interested in and can articulate to others. Students may also give impromptu talks to peers to review understanding of the concept learned that day. Expert groups may be discussing a project topic while preparing to present to the class. Volunteers can offer to review the answers on the daily class assignment with a partner.

When students, especially those with risk factors, begin to take charge of learning activities in class, you will see them gaining self-esteem, producing improved products, and giving and receiving immediate feedback that reinforces their capabilities and strengths, which they so desire.

Presentations may be given by an individual, by partners, or in groups while the student audience supports and encourages the speaker(s) to do well.

Empowerment and ownership of learning is amplified by peer validation and appreciation. When the speakers finish, students may cheer and offer praise and constructive criticism so that the student(s) will continue to grow and improve. The presenters feel accomplished and enthusiastic because they mastered the content.

For example, when students choose a topic in which they are interested and connect that to the concepts and content they are learning, they are more likely to sustain engagement even if the work becomes challenging. Students' commitment to project work can be quite impressive when the dots connect for them from their interests to the curriculum for which a teacher is responsible.

For example, a middle school student, one who had not been successful in school, became incredibly interested in how to build a tech-based project that would train pitchers to throw strikes. He developed a prototype frame and tested and retested the laser matrix he was using to trigger LED lights on the board—green for a strike, red for a ball. The school year ended, and he continued working on the project. He worked on the project in the summer and came back to school motivated to develop an improved version of the original. What did he learn in the project? He learned so much about communication as he built a website and began to use Twitter to publicize his project. He created a business plan and pitched his project at a start-up weekend. He won the start-up pitch, and from there his project took off as he continued to make improvements and work on patenting his project (Glinska 2015).

We have come to understand that the narrative of learning can be different for each student, which is why we believe in the value of finding a context that allows each learner to make connections. We let our students find activities in the daily agenda and work on those at different paces and in different places. Some students will be at the most basic level of what we plan to teach that day, and other students will already have deeper background knowledge from researching, reading, or writing about the topic. Students know we support them to move forward.

The teacher is moving from student-to-student inquiring about the concepts taught that day. The teacher can inquire about previous days' lessons as well, or even into the future. Wherever a student is on the learning spectrum, the teacher moves that student forward toward growth and achievement, using a variety of techniques and through a variety of technological devices. If students need to type their writing or science projects, because it is more efficient, allow time for this to occur.

Each student is engaged throughout the class time. The activities switch about every fifteen or twenty minutes. The teacher has a constant pulse on each student. He or she is ready to move each student forward in the learning process. How does the teacher keep track of this?

There are many resources available to keep record. Often, the teacher maintains a Google Doc, spreadsheet, or a composition book, a page or two per student with the background and academic information. This book remains in the teacher's hands or in a locked cabinet. The composition book is full of knowledge regarding each student's strengths, needs, interests, academic progress, learning style, and notes about what works with that student and what to avoid. Each child gets his or her own learning plan, pace, and choice of grouping.

Other teachers might choose to keep an online record for each student. There are many online note-taking options. The student creates a Google Folder, titled that year or grade. This folder will contain numerous folders titled with the various areas of that curriculum. This will be the student's "digital portfolio." The student shares with the teacher, and the teacher will monitor the progress for each student while also using it to comment on any important student documents.

TALKING WITH STUDENTS

Cheryl routinely schedules opportunities for students to personally share what they have learned during the course of a unit. Conferences with students are key to knowing what they have learned and what they still need to learn. When Cheryl begins to move about the room, sitting down to check in with students, they have learned to quietly wait in anticipation of a conference with the teacher. She has found that they look forward to talking about what they know. She typically frames her student progress conferences with three questions:

1. What do you think has been important to learn so far and why?
2. What challenges have you run into as you have been working on your project, and what can I do to help you with those?
3. How have you used feedback to get what you need to make sure this is your best work?

Michael says that every student is a teacher and every teacher is a student. As he works with a student, he describes himself as often learning more from that student than he could have imagined. For example, in a conference, a student might discuss types of ecosystems, longitude and latitude, what body system is used to digest food, or types of characters in the novel he or she is reading.

Individual conferences help you make connections and build relationships with students (Spencer 2015). Most adolescents love to talk, especially when they are given a purpose for speaking. As the teacher, your role is to listen and record information to help you consider the next steps you need to take to support the student. However, even as you use a composition book or a Google Doc to make notes during the conference, it is important to look the student in the eye and listen to answers to the questions you ask.

When you conference with students, they realize you care enough to want to engage with them about their learning. Conferences provide students with an opportunity to take a risk to share what has gone well or not so well in their work. You can set the stage by sharing that this is a time for both of you to figure out what is interesting or challenging about the work the student is doing and that your job is to help.

When you debrief in a one-to-one conference with a student, you may pick up on whether a student needs additional intervention. Does this student understand the concepts taught, or does he or she need additional practice, or enrichment? This could be as simple as needing some extra time with you to address small learning gaps. Or, there could be a need for intervention services such as speech assistance, guidance, or glasses.

Sometimes in conferences, students can articulate what they understand and when they are ready to move forward. Sometimes, a student says they understand, and then you may have a conversation with that student and they know nothing about the events in the novel they are reading. They may just be reading the words but not processing them.

You will then know to proceed by trying different instructional strategies to help the student connect better with the content. Sometimes students need to have access to a text-to-speech application so they can hear words while tracking print with their eyes. You might also need to assess their comprehension with a tool such as the Qualitative Reading Inventory ("Informal Reading Inventory [Qualitative Reading Inventory]" 2013) to determine if you need to vary the levels of books the student is reading in class. You also may need to add some additional time with the student to provide some scaffolding support through comprehension strategy focus (Adler, n.d.).

What are other students doing while you are sitting next to a student conversing and listening? Students know how to move forward and delve deeper into their work plan even if you are not available all the time. It is not only students identified as gifted who are allowed to move forward. Because they have a plan, students know what to do next or they can ask "three before me!"

With each action you take in class, we believe it is important to keep one question front and center: "What is best for this student?" In your notes that reflect ideas, suggestions, conversations, knowledge of content, strengths, needs, and interests of each student, you will gain insights into each student that will inform your work as a professional to be sure that all in your class are afforded access to equitable resources, the time they need from you, and the differentiated opportunities to ensure learning success.

SAMPLE LESSON AND "MAKER" TIME

What does making look like in a middle school classroom? There are tubs and carts full of materials that students can use to build, create, and manipulate. The teacher places tubs on tables and explains how each can be utilized. The timer is set, students move to whichever tub interests them, and they begin to create. The focus is on the item and not who is in your group. All students are engaged.

During formal writing time, students use the creation cart or tech tools to create or make something before they begin to write. Engaging in "maker" time prior to writing helps students clear their minds so that they are able to write. A student may have had a bad morning because of losing an item, or an argument with a family member. When creating and making, they tend to get into a flow and forget all else as they build or construct.

How do you obtain maker items in the middle school setting? You can ask for donations at Back-to-School Night or at student orientation. You can buy kits with PTO money or department money and keep them stocked with parent donations. There are always parents who want to be involved and don't know where to begin. Ask them to come to a maker session, and they will see how quickly the materials are utilized.

You may want to try to convince your librarian to set up a mobile maker cart in the library so that more teachers can begin to utilize maker time in class. For example, this would allow you to sign out a cart of craft items, wires and electrical circuit building items, LED lights, Legos, and other building materials from the media center. Teachers can then rotate these carts weekly and create a list for the media specialist as to what needs restocked.

Making is an important part of the schools where Cheryl and Michael work. They've discovered that students need to build and create. Once finished, their minds are ready to start on their work. Making something as part of the day's agenda can lead to both great fiction and nonfiction writing, solutions to math equations, or beginning to develop an ecosystem project (Moran 2017).

INTEGRATING READING AND WRITING

After the timer sounds, the students know they have two minutes to clean up and replace maker tubs on the cart. They then open their laptops or device of choice and begin writing. The fingers are flying across the keyboards as fast as lightning. They allow their thoughts to race as they place their ideas on the page.

At the beginning of the year, writing assignments should be open-ended choice or simple topics. Allow students success in writing before you begin getting more in depth with writing lessons. Allow them to place their thoughts, the way they choose, onto the paper. They can either write or type.

After several days have passed at the beginning of the year, you can then begin to discuss forms of writing with students. A good start is getting them to demonstrate in their writing that stories have a beginning, middle, and end. When you introduce a new writing lesson, use graphic organizers such as a plot diagram or story map to help students make sense of what they are writing—and reading (Gonzalez 2017). Visual representations are an important strategy to help students make sense of learning. In fact, visual representations are critical to implementing universal design for learning (UDL).

Allow students, at times, the freedom to choose writing genres. Providing the option of personal narratives or creative writing lead adolescent writers to stories of their choice. Writing about what they know ultimately engages them in the writing process. Reluctant writers will write of experiences hunting with their fathers or of working on the farm. Another student may want to write a fictionalized piece about a skateboarder, drawing upon his or her own experiences.

After maker time, students should write for about twelve to fifteen minutes daily. Students usually ask for additional time. This is a good time to let them know they are welcome to write at any time that they are in Google Documents, which they can access always. They may also utilize tablets, or even write in a writer's notebook. This is their choice.

Students may ask if they can integrate stories with those of other students, either in your class or in another class. Writing takes many forms. The teacher moves about the room conferencing with students using probing questions: What type of character is this? Who is the protagonist in your story? Who else is writing with you? Where is the section of this piece that you wrote? The teacher can then work on grammar, parts of speech, spelling, and other standards, one on one with each student.

There are times that the teacher has the students set their own writing aside and assigns a choice of one of three writing prompts. All students will use the prompts as a starting point. The students begin going through a process of brainstorming, prewriting, rough drafting, peer editing, and finally editing for their final copy. The teacher views the writing and offers comments, either orally or via comments in Google Docs, and the students continue to make revisions. This strategy repeats itself through the writing process.

Some students like to be praised publicly and some quietly. You can ask students to share with you their preferences for receiving feedback whether to give praise when it is warranted or suggestions to improve writing as well. It's always a good idea to model sharing an authentically positive statement prior to feedback about areas for improvement. You might say, "I like that you used character dialogue in this writing assignment, especially

_____." After discussion about the dialogue, you can add, "I'd also like to talk about how you can add details to your writing."

Then as you leave, you might make a quick note on your cell phone or in your journal to check back in later to follow up. This doesn't happen without making it systemic to your facilitation of learning in a more personalized way. That means finding and allocating precious time to extend the feedback and conference conversation cycle.

How do you find the time at the beginning of class each day or at class changes to touch base with individual students and just check in on notes such as you may have recorded about adding writing details? Many teachers begin class with a "do now" activity that previews new content or reviews prior content. This can be a sentence that a student labels using parts of speech or a math problem introducing a new topic of instruction. A "do now" can also be a review of the previous day's instruction. A student completes this and transitions to a quiet activity such as reading or writing.

This gives you the opportunity to move around to check in with students to make sure they are internalizing a story they are reading by utilizing reading strategies. You can ask as many of the students as possible, "What reading strategy are you using right now?" You can also question students about concepts such as protagonist/antagonist that they are learning to help them understand the theme of a novel as well as establishing a story theme in their writing. It's your time to follow up on specific feedback that you have shared to help a student take next steps in improving his or her work.

Making connections with students also occurs by asking them questions when conferencing with them. Your connections are essential with students so that they feel you are trustworthy. To start that process, you might conduct "getting to know you" activities or team-building activities such as class meetings by having students convene in a circle, greet each other, share news, discuss a concept/idea, and then follow it with an activity. Set up an environment where it is okay to pass on responding to a question or sharing with others.

You can also demonstrate and model compassion and make a connection when a student/class tells you about an incident that they feel needs to be discussed and resolved, with a response such as, "Thank you for sharing that. We need to figure out what we can do to address that concern." It's also a time when you are building connections when you can model writing with students who may not want to publicly or verbally discuss something they want you to know. Just be sure that if you can't comfortably address a concern, consult with the school counselor or administrator.

Each student needs to have at least one teacher in whom they can confide. To create an environment and culture in which all learners feel valued, you will need to always keep a focus on strategies to build trust, respect, and an open but structured atmosphere so students will feel they can take a risk in that class. They will learn and utilize that knowledge as a lifelong learner, knowing how to learn, preparing themselves for the workforce. Students will learn in a trusting and respectful environment, where there are choices to be made and the student can make those choices often.

We have been so amazed to see a student, over the course of the school year, change from being the shy student, angry student, noncompliant student, or disengaged student. The most important strategy we have discovered to help us continue to keep working toward solutions even when a student challenges our competencies has been to have a critical friend, a colleague with whom we can talk and reflect upon different strategies and approaches to working with a student who is struggling.

We encourage you to find that friend in your school. If you don't forge a relationship with a peer in your school, look outside to other district schools or even to chats on Twitter ("Cybraryman Internet Catalogue," n.d.). Whether its #ntchat for new teachers or #hacklearning chat for educators working to change practice, you can develop close bonds and relationships with teachers all over the world on topics of importance to you and ultimately, of help to the students you teach.

WORKS CITED

Adler, C. R. n.d. "Seven Strategies to Teach Students Text Comprehension." AdLit. Accessed July 8, 2018. http://www.adlit.org/article/3479/.

"Cybraryman Internet Catalogue." n.d. Cybraryman.com. Accessed July 8, 2018. https://cybraryman.com/chats.html.

Glinska, Gosia. 2015. "From Class Clown To CEO: How Entrepreneurship Education Benefits K-12 Students." *Forbes Magazine*, November 9, 2015. https://www.forbes.com/sites/darden/2015/11/09/from-class-clown-to-ceo-how-entrepreneurship-education-benefits-k-12-students/.

Gonzalez, Jennifer. 2017. "The Great and Powerful Graphic Organizer." Cult of Pedagogy. October 22, 2017. https://www.cultofpedagogy.com/graphic-organizer/.

"Informal Reading Inventory (Qualitative Reading Inventory)." 2013. Reading Rockets. April 24, 2013. http://www.readingrockets.org/article/informal-reading-inventory-qualitative-reading-inventory.

Moran, Pam. 2017. "When Kids Make." *A Space for Learning* (blog). July 24, 2017. https://spacesforlearning.wordpress.com/2017/07/24/when-kids-make/.

Socol, Ira David. 2012. "Re-thinking the Middle School." *SpeEd Change* (blog). March 11, 2012. http://speedchange.blogspot.com/2012/03/re-thinking-middle-school.html.

Spencer, John. 2015. "The Power of Student Conferencing." *John Spencer* (blog). April 9, 2015. http://www.spencerauthor.com/the-power-of-student-conferencing/.

Chapter Sixteen

High School Learning Spaces

The past is gone forever, and the future —the Smart Machine Age—is happening faster and faster.—Edward Hess

QUESTIONS TO PONDER IN THIS CHAPTER

- *If high schools of today serve learners with different characteristics and needs than learners of the last two decades, what changes are needed to support those learners?*
- *What do we understand about today's workforce and communities that leads high schools to need to change?*
- *In what ways might high school teachers get started thinking about redesign of high school learning spaces?*

THE NATURE OF HIGH SCHOOL AND TODAY'S TEENS

In a *Time* magazine article in December 2006, the article's authors hypothesized that if Rip Van Winkle awoke in the twenty-first century, he wouldn't recognize much from his prior life—unless he walked into a school. There, he would know exactly where he was (Wallace and Steptoe 2006). However, some schools are committed to not being Rip Van Winkle schools.

Walk into one high school on any given day and you might see very different spaces and learning in progress. In a library's music studio, a couple of students work on beat machines, staring at a screen on which sound graphs change as their beats slow, speed, or change tone. A few other students are gathered in a corner of the studio and armed with guitars and a drum kit, playing and replaying riffs until they transition into a bit of music from their grandparents' generation.

A young woman talks to her teacher about rap lyrics she is drafting for a song she will record that tells the story of her life. In the hallway outside the studio, a few teens lounge on wooden benches, their laptops plugged into charging bars that have replaced the lockers that once occupied every square inch of wall space. They are working on a community project to create a local website version of Humans of New York. Next door, a team-taught humanities class is circled up in a variety of chairs discussing the book *A Long Walk to Water*.

Some of the students in the group are immigrants who are sharing their own context for what it means to live in a place where no one takes an abundance of water for granted. It's hard to tell as the teachers guide the conversation whether history or English is the focus of the unit design. In fact, it's both. The outcome in this school, or the end in mind, is tied to a profile of a graduate that identifies critical thinking, collaborative teamwork, problem solving, health and wellness, creative production, and citizenship as well as knowledge as key to what they need to be successful in life after high school.

These scenes are not outliers in schools where contemporary learning is based more on competency development than content acquisition. The learning community in such schools continuously studies how the world is changing around them and their students. Rather than sustaining the educational status quo, teachers who seek to understand implications of the "smart machine age" know that curriculum must be flexible, tool use constantly evolving, and they themselves agile in adapting new instructional strategies to meet the learning needs of students in this century.

High school educators have different challenges than elementary and middle school educators do. The learners they teach begin high school at fourteen, and by graduation most qualify as adults leaving to attend college, go to work, take a gap year, or enter the military. High school graduation depends upon students passing a wide range of required courses and tests, and their teachers are responsible for making that happen.

Yet much of what high school students are required to do lacks relevance and makes little sense to them in terms of application to today's life goals. Programs that traditionally engaged teens, such as shop, marketing, the visual and performing arts, and so much more, have been whittled down in scope and offering, especially for learners at risk of graduating who find themselves double- and even triple-blocked into remediation essential to earning a diploma.

High school teachers of this century are challenged to engage the contemporary teenagers they teach in relevant learning, while also ensuring they meet external standards for graduation. Doing both is a challenge, but one that can be met.

We know this because there are high schools reimagining and changing learning spaces all over the country. However, most have a long way to go in creating the quality and depth of changes necessary to prepare young people for the coming decades.

WHY CHANGE LEARNING SPACES?

Changing teaching places to learning spaces presents unique challenges in high schools because there is no area of K–12 public education where pedagogy is as static. Teachers must cover extraordinary amounts of content to meet standards, and the dominant form of teaching remains mostly at the board with print-based assignments in and out of class. However, if engaging high school learners is an expectation, then space redesign also must be accompanied by a significant commitment to pedagogical shifts in practice (not to mention curriculum and assessment).

The teen brain is an active mind searching for meaning, seeking patterns and connections, and welcoming challenges to think creatively and critically. Teens value social learning communities both face-to-face and virtual—and the use of devices to stay connected with the world to share their experiences.

They appreciate teachers who build relationships with them. Yet when teens walk into high schools each day, they often are required to power down. For them, that means powering down friends, their devices, and even their active minds as they take passive seats to listen to teachers or work on written assignments day after day.

Changing the traditional model of teaching and learning that dominates high school today has never been so essential to ensuring that young people are ready for life after graduation. Students need to have routine opportunities to engage with peers in project work that develops and sustains creativity, problem solving, and a wide span of planning and research skills.

They need to develop broad communication skills using a variety of forms of tools and media while also learning to negotiate the increasing complex world of social media they have been using since elementary school ("Using Twitter to Promote Learning" 2015). Teens must develop deep metacognitive behaviors that push them to think about how they learn, make decisions and reflect upon outcomes, and organize their thinking.

High school students need to have fewer constraints and more breadth in project work so that they can range outside the prescribed curricula as they find, explore, and connect their own interests and passions to what they are expected to learn as well as what they want to learn.

They need to learn to use their devices not just for entertainment and social purposes, but more importantly for learning purposes. When this becomes the context of learning for teens, their engagement levels go up and they are more likely to willingly come back to school every day with an interest in the work they do.

Teachers who value engaging teen learners recognize that their interests must be brought into the context of the high school curriculum. This happens when teachers set up situations for students to work and converse with each other at higher levels of Bloom's taxonomy. Such teachers listen and ask questions of teens that push them to consider how they can bring their ideas, skills, and talents into project work. They work to develop relationships and know how to draw students' interests and curiosity into the learning.

Principals in high schools with a mission to engage all learners also look for ways to alter the experiences of teens by creating a range of options that open multiple pathways to teen engagement. This could result in opening a music construction studio in the library, a makerspace in the science area, or collaborative work spaces in lobby areas throughout the school.

They also support teachers who want to try out different ways to design learning experiences from story-based world language learning to case-study-driven history classes. They see capstone projects as a way for seniors to demonstrate portfolio accomplishments to peers and the community.

In addition, principals and teachers who are committed to learners' engagement see why integrated curricula appeal to teens' need to make sense of course content. Math courses taught in isolation of any real-world, science, or historical contexts makes little sense to teens.

The English/language arts canon that lacks diversity and modern-day relevance simply becomes a path to websites where students can download answers to the normative questions about books of the past. Science and social studies without inquiry are a series of disconnected lectures and low-level tests with an occasional video thrown in to interrupt passivity in the classroom.

But all hope is not lost for high school engagement of learners, however, for all over the nation, there are current and expanding examples of schools in which staff have changed the paradigm for courses taught in isolation and who now as staff plan and even coteach interdisciplinary content. In such schools, content begins to make sense. Learners see school as a space for learning, not just a place where they are required to show up and hopefully do.

MAKING THE SHIFT

In high schools across the country, teachers and principals are changing the environment and instruction to provide choices in seating that are comfortable options. They are moving single desks and rigid chairs out and bringing tables and flex chairs in. They are finding as they offer differently designed seating that high schoolers also appreciate working together at a variety of heights from tall cafe spaces to traditional tables.

High schoolers also like to sink into soft-seating couches tucked into a classroom nook or corner where they can work quietly or read with a friend. They like being able to move and change positions as they work—a test of

the teacher's flexibility and instructional tolerance for students owning choices.

Teachers who believe they make a difference with teens tend to embrace changes in seating and environmental design because they value students working together and pursuing content standards through interest-driven projects. They want teens in their classes to succeed and care about their work, indeed, to own their own learning, and to see themselves as possessing the agency of self-directedness.

As a result, they also are more willing to shift from teacher-centric environments to learner-centered spaces and to embrace pedagogies of project-based learning, interactive and production-oriented technology applications, and connectivity that brings knowledge and skill expertise to students from sources other than the teacher or print-based text.

The essence of changing spaces in high school lies in these pedagogical shifts that teachers make. Otherwise, schools simply bring new furniture in, add some new technologies, and maybe move some classes around, but in the end nothing will have changed for the learners. To create a space for risk, both pedagogy and environment must shift just as it must in middle and elementary school (Thornton and Harris 2015).

That's why the hard work of changing spaces must begin with the even harder work of changing practices of asking questions, and researching contemporary practices that prepare students for life after high school is critical in the process of changing spaces. High school teachers who build deep understanding of changes in the workforce and communities today begin to see strategies that engage learners in content differently.

They see inquiry, seminar, case studies, and project- and problem-based learning as key to students acquiring lifelong learning competencies, not just content knowledge. This means shifting from strategies that promote surface learning to those that cement deep learning and transfer (Juliani 2014).

WHAT'S POSSIBLE? HIGH SCHOOL LEARNING SPACES

If shifting practices can occur in a high school, what are some possibilities for altering space to support those shifts? Shifts begin with a sense of vision and design that takes into account contemporary learners and what we know about their brains. High school students have a drive for greater autonomy than at any time perhaps since they were toddlers. They can be impulsive decision makers, and they almost always have a high-powered tool in their pocket to help them quickly react and respond to the environment around them as they make decisions.

Teachers have to roam what we know about the teen brain and learning before they begin to design spaces, whether it's the library, science labs, classrooms, or hallways. Some design principles that can lead to deep faculty discussions about the learning space needs of teens include the following:

- *Connectivity* of today's learners to each other and the world is a given in learning spaces.
- For all students to achieve success, they must have *universal access* to tools and *interactive* technologies that support them as individual learners and in teams.
- Students need *choice and comfort* in learning spaces to work together and individually. Because of unique differences among learners, options in seating are key to providing a continuum of learning environments in class and the school that allow active movement.
- Differentiation of learning spaces must be considered through a lens of how each space is designed to maximize *flexibility* in use—in seating options, in tabletop space, how walls are used, ease of movement of furniture, electrical access for tools, resource access, and storage, and project production areas.
- *Transparency* of classrooms is key. Whenever possible, natural lighting and the capability to focus the eye for distant vision is essential to avoiding eye strain caused by intense focus on pages or screens.
- High school offers opportunities for learners to gather for informal learning—libraries, hallways, cafeterias, classrooms, courtyards, and more.

CHANGES THAT SOME HIGH SCHOOLS HAVE MADE

High school staff across the nation have made changes in space as a result of auditing where students gather together or like to work by themselves, their interests beyond the prescribed curricula, classroom observations, and survey and focus group information about their levels of engagement. They also have researched and used information about the teen brain, changes in the workforce and community diversity, and strategies that effectively engage learners. In their research, school goals and priorities have been set beyond simply getting high schoolers through the courses and tests they need to graduate (Dobbs and Cahana 2011).

They have been willing to take risks and try new approaches to learning and to involve students in the process of making changes by honoring their different perspectives about what teens need from their high school "user experience."

Such changes include:

- Removal of lockers and replacement with hallway bench seating and charging bars for devices

- Reimagination of libraries into learning commons with makerspaces, student-run help desks, project design studios, cafe areas, music construction studios, movable bookcases, projection areas with headsets for individual or small-group use of the internet or video streaming, VR stations, and tool kits for checkout
- Creation of flexible learning options in classroom environments—couches, cafe tables, large standing tables for group work, soft-seating chairs for small-group gathering, drop-down electrical outlets, multiuse walls that can be used for large project design work by students, and movable projection devices for use by students and teachers
- Redesign of lab spaces in science with mobile workbenches and tables, multiple sinks, flexible storage cabinets, and high-density electrical and charging bar connections for devices
- Development of "caves, campfires, and watering holes" coteaching spaces (single and double-plus classroom options) designed for interdisciplinary and collaborative teaching and learning that include round tables, flexible seating arrangements, and gathering areas that accommodate whole- and small-group work as well as individual learning options
- Addition of fitness areas and equipment that can be incorporated into the learning commons, and classroom or gym areas for use by students informally or formally in activities from yoga to treadmill walking
- Delineation of hallways and lobby areas with enough space to create small-group study or project work areas for students using tables and/or flexible seating arrangements
- Redesign of the cafeteria to create a flexible dining and cafe experience that may run on an extended schedule so that students can choose to eat when they need and want to do so based on their school release times—study hall, project activities in class, et cetera
- Creation of informal and formal presentation spaces in the library, lobbies, or formal theater areas for students to perform, stage projects, or engage in activities such as slam poetry or sharing music

THE OPEN MIND-SET DILEMMA

This kind of change in high schools will not occur without staff who have an open mind-set to considering new ways of working with teens, including flexible scheduling, interdisciplinary learning, project-based learning, student activity and talk, use of technologies to power up learning experiences and differentiated options, and opportunities that address access and equity needs of all learners. Mind-sets that are fixed will tend to reinforce status quo and reject changes in practice or space. There are good reasons why high school educators resist shifts in teaching. After all, high school is the highest stakes of all learning environments.

High school staff face the dilemma every day of "If I take the time to engage learners and use PBL, they may not pass the state tests they need to graduate. But if I don't take the time to engage them, then the learning they do is on the surface and won't stick. Some still won't pass state tests." This dilemma is one that lives in the halls of high schools and won't change until externally imposed testing abates. However, that doesn't mean that high school staff can't make changes that are needed. They just need more time to process through and mitigate risks associated with change.

High school educators need to know how proposed changes will make a difference in preparing learning for life after graduation. Before changes will occur, they need to be convinced that changes will help learners achieve by any measure or metric of success. They need to first understand the purpose of proposed changes before they will embrace them. They need to know that building leaders will support them with professional development that makes sense, the tools they need to implement changes, and a willingness to support the risks inherent in changing space and practice.

Change does not come easily to staff who are steeped in the traditions of twentieth-century command and control, cells and bells schooling. However, there are great examples of high schools that have reimagined and designed both spaces and pedagogies for educating teens in this century. Those range from large comprehensive to private to alternative high schools. Some have fully shifted, and others are in progress (Vander Ark 2013). However, being open to changes that serve Generation Z teens well is the critical disposition of high schools that work for all learners and learning versus simply replicating schools of the past.

How will you help make the essential changes that your high school needs? How might you change one thing using this chapter? How might you document the impact such a change may have on learners and learning?

WORKS CITED

Dobbs, David, and Kitra Cahana. 2011. "Teenage Brains." *National Geographic*, October 1, 2011. https://www.nationalgeographic.com/magazine/2011/10/beautiful-brains/.

Juliani, A. J. 2014. "10 Commandments of Innovative Teaching." *A. J. Juliani* (blog). January 23, 2014. http://ajjuliani.com/10-commandments-innovative-teaching/.

Thornton, Michael, and Cheryl Harris. 2015. "Creating Space for Risk." Edutopia. George Lucas Educational Foundation. 2015. https://www.edutopia.org/blog/creating-space-for-risk-michael-thornton-cheryl-harris.

"Using Twitter to Promote Learning." 2015. Edutopia. George Lucas Educational Foundation. July 8, 2015. https://www.edutopia.org/practice/social-media-making-connections-through-twitter.

Vander Ark, Tom. 2013. "35 High Schools Worth Visiting." *Education Week*, November 13, 2013. http://blogs.edweek.org/edweek/on_innovation/2013/11/35_high_schools_worth_visiting.html.

Wallace, Claudia, and Wanda Steptoe. 2006. "How to Bring Our Schools Out of the 20th Century." *Time*, December 9, 2006.http://content.time.com/time/nation/article/0,8599,1568429,00.html.

About the Authors

Ira David Socol joined Albemarle County Public Schools (ACPS) in Charlottesville, Virginia, in 2013 in support of the division's Design 2015 initiative, which focused on project-based and collaborative learning programs across schools. A year later, he became the division's assistant director of educational technology. In that role, he shaped the installation of software packages on student computers adaptable to individual learning styles and needs. Examples include multiple text-to-speech reading and speech-to-text dictation programs, multiple calculators, and creative tools for art and music. He also helped develop strategies for teachers to engage learners through interactive technologies, connectivity, project/problem/passion-based learning, and student choice and comfort in the classroom.

Ira was selected in 2017 by the Center for Digital Education, a national organization whose mission is to "nurture a community of thought leaders who are rethinking education with technology as the catalyst," as one of its thirty top technologists, transformers, and trailblazers. He is known internationally for his "toolbelt theory," a systemic approach to providing universal design for learning, and has presented his research on globally open technology and contemporary learning spaces.

He has taught at Michigan State and Grand Valley State Universities and at Pratt Institute. He also was a consultant for assistive technology for Michigan's Vocational Rehabilitation Agency. He received his bachelor of arts from Grand Valley State University and holds certifications in assistive technology from the University of California at Northridge and in employment training from Michigan State University.

Cheryl (Walchack) Harris is a seventh-grade language arts teacher of thirty-five years, currently in the Albemarle County School System in Charlottesville, Virginia. She taught grades five through twelve always in the surrounding area of Charlottesville. She is a native of West Springfield, Pennsylvania, and draws numerous ideas for instruction from her childhood experiences and through proven research. She is a true believer of always gaining new knowledge, innovation, creativity, tolerance, compassion, empathy, open-door communication, collaboration, and connecting with both her current and former students and letting them know that she is truly passionate about their growth in education and being productive members of society.

She has coauthored an article, had it published, and has also been featured in a video regarding flexible classrooms with Edutopia. Cheryl has led numerous professional development sessions, both at conferences and at schools, regarding differentiation, student-led conferences, best practice strategies that work in the classroom, how to include all students every day in your lessons, and many more.

Her passion blossoms when teaching at the county's annual summer Coder Dojo. This involves collaborating with lead technology instructors and teachers for the purpose of instructing students ages five through sixteen with coding activities such as Minecraft, Kodu, Scratch, 3D-printing, and other innovative topics. Cheryl has been lead teacher for the Language Arts Department and served on school improvement committees at Sutherland Middle School. She was also chair of the Teacher Advisory Committee for ACPS, who meets with the deputy superintendent of schools to assist in making positive changes in the schools.

Cheryl maintains a desire to improve not only schools but the community around her. She continues to serve as chair of the chief's Crime Prevention Council and on the Citizen's Advisory Committee of the Albemarle County Police Department, Charlottesville, Virginia. She believes in giving back and helping when she can.

Besides spending time with her two children and their spouses, three grandchildren, five grand fur babies, and two kitties, she loves spending time at the beach, reading, writing, working in her flower beds, and spending time with other family members and friends.

Cheryl has her master of education degree in administration, supervision, and curriculum K–12 through the University of Virginia, Charlottesville, and her bachelor of science degree in education from Clarion University, Clarion, Pennsylvania.

J. Michael Thornton II has been an educator for fourteen years in the Albemarle County/Charlottesville, Virginia, area. He has an undergraduate degree in history, a master of arts in teaching, and a master of education in administration and supervision. He has taught kindergarten as well as second, third, fourth, and fifth grade.

Michael helped open a new K–5 flexible multiage learning space for 120 students in a six-hundred-student school. He is passionate about learning and about helping students find their passions and interests. Lastly, his dedication to project- and passion-based learning aligned with digital integration and making has enabled him to see the power and importance of taking risks in the classroom. In addition to teaching in an elementary setting, Michael teaches undergraduate and graduate courses at Mary Baldwin University and Piedmont Virginia Community College. Currently, Michael is an assistant principal intern.

Michael has been married for fourteen years and is blessed to have three beautiful kids. He loves spending time with his family. He is always thankful for the consistent support his family offers him.

www.ingramcontent.com/pod-product-compliance
Lightning Source LLC
Chambersburg PA
CBHW020739230426
43665CB00009B/496